Praise for *Breaking the Rules*

"*Breaking the Rules* will be like a defibrillator on many hearts which are more dead than alive and restorative to many souls that are lost in the maze of religion rather than a life-giving relationship with a loving God. Fil Anderson has extended an invitation to live outside the box of religion. I hope you will accept it. If you are more 'churched' than transformed, then this book is for you!"

Stephen W. Smith, author of *The Lazarus Life* and *The Transformation of a Man's Heart*

"With precision, patience and vulnerability Fil beckons us to let go of the life-crushing burdens of religion in exchange for the freedom of God's reckless love."

Nathan Foster, author of *Wisdom Chaser*

"By unveiling the authentic Jesus—One more true to the biblical witness than the religious rule-abiding killjoy whom too many of our churches have inadvertently endorsed—Fil Anderson opens readers' eyes to the unbridled goodness of the God who knows us and loves us exactly as we are. Anderson's message is irresistible!"

Margot Starbuck, author of *The Girl in the Orange Dress*

"Few words are as misused today as *intimacy*. Break it down and to most people it means 'into me I see.' Fil Anderson shows us not only how the word really breaks down—'you're invited into a relational encounter with God'—he also shows us how to embrace the one thing our hearts desire most."

Leonard Sweet, author of *So Beautiful: Divine Designs for Life and the Church*

"Finally, relief for tired and weary souls. Fil leads leaders to an intimacy with Jesus that does not require unbending rule-keeping. Written with honesty and compassion, readers can identify with Fil's own struggles and have reason to hope that they too can plunge into the depths of God's love for us. If you are ready to experience intimacy, freedom and grace, this is the book for you."

Tom Wilson, president and CEO, OneHundredX, Leadership Network and Halftime

"*Breaking the Rules* captures the essence of what makes Christianity impossible—and how a wild, unpredictable but authentic relationship with Jesus is the only cure for what ails us. Bracingly honest, these pages will haunt you in the best way possible. I recommend you read them slowly . . . and savor."

Paula Rinehart, author of *Strong Women, Soft Hearts*

BREAKING
THE RULES

Trading Performance for Intimacy with God

Fil Anderson

Foreword by Brennan Manning

IVP Books

An imprint of InterVarsity Press
Downers Grove, Illinois

InterVarsity Press
P.O. Box 1400, Downers Grove, IL 60515-1426
World Wide Web: www.ivpress.com
E-mail: email@ivpress.com

InterVarsity Press® is the book-publishing division of InterVarsity Christian Fellowship/USA®, a
movement of students and faculty active on campus at hundreds of universities, colleges and schools
of nursing in the United States of America, and a member movement of the International Fellowship
of Evangelical Students. For information about local and regional activities, write Public Relations
Dept., InterVarsity Christian Fellowship/USA, 6400 Schroeder Rd., P.O. Box 7895, Madison, WI
53707-7895, or visit the IVCF website at <www.intervarsity.org>.

Scripture quotations, unless otherwise noted, are from The Message. Copyright © 1993, 1994, 1995.
Used by permission of NavPress Publishing Group. All rights reserved.

Design: Cindy Kiple

Images: chessboard background: Duncan Walker/iStockphoto
      chess pieces, white and black knights: Anton Seleznev/iStockphoto
      galloping horse: Kseniya Abramova/iStockphoto

ISBN 978-0-8308-3537-9

Printed in the United States of America ∞

Library of Congress Cataloging-in-Publication Data

Anderson, Fil.
  Breaking the rules: trading performance for intimacy with God / Fil
Anderson.
    p. cm.
  Includes bibliographical references.
  ISBN 978-0-8308-3537-9 (cloth: alk. paper)
  1. Spirituality. I. Title.
  BV4501.3.A524 2009
  248.4—dc22

                                               2009042066

P	18	17	16	15	14	13	12	11	10	9	8	7	6	5	4	3	2	1
Y	25	24	23	22	21	20	19	18	17	16	15	14	13	12	11	10

To the memory of three individuals who,
by their example, taught me more about
how to break the rules than any other
people I've encountered:

The first-century lady who anointed Jesus with perfume

Mike Yaconelli

Paul Barclay

Contents

Foreword

I've known Fil Anderson for twenty-five years. We met during a conference in Vail, Colorado, where I was speaking. At the time we were both desperately insecure men, total strangers to each other. While sharing with me the gift of his vulnerability, my heart was ravished by his scorching honesty and humble transparency. During those memorable days one of the few deep friendships I have ever had in my life began. I've never doubted that our meeting was by divine appointment. Looking back, there is simply no other reasonable explanation.

Meanwhile, on numerous occasions, I've acknowledged how my critics complain that I write too much about the wild, unrestricted love of God and not enough about sin and judgment and hell and how to keep Christ in Christmas. They maintain that I am unbalanced, unsound and a little bit crazy. While I have never hesitated to plead guilty to that last charge, I have remained confident that God would raise up other unbalanced, unsound and crazy writers to cry with me the scandalous truth of the gospel of Jesus Christ:

> *God loves you as you are, not as you should be,*
> *since no one is the person they should be.*

This fiercely bold and honest book has renewed my hope and secured my confidence that I don't cry this message alone. *Break-*

ing the Rules heralds the shattering truth that the transcendent God who became visible in Jesus Christ furiously longs for intimacy with us. It assures worn-out and weary religious strivers that their life can be recovered. It dispatches many of the groundless substitutions, deviations and distortions of Jesus' original offer of friendship and clearly points the way to a life of freedom from religion-induced guilt.

Fil's appeal to people caught in the deadly web of religious self-help is personal and impassioned, reminding me of the apostle Paul's fiery enunciation, "You stupid Galatians!" As well as anyone I know, Fil understands the dangers that exist for those who prostitute the gospel—telling lies about God and making Jesus more of a law-giver than an unconditional lover. He writes: "The pathology of my religion erupted in insidious fashion: believing and doing the right things became a *substitute* for living in right relationship with God. As a result, I got lost in the details and simultaneously lost my heart. I spent most of my time learning what I *couldn't* do instead of celebrating and enjoying what I *could* do because of my relationship with Jesus."

His portrayal of the brokenness in his life is achingly beautiful. Fil writes: "For years shame, deception, lies, betrayals, relationship breakdowns, disappointments, and unresolved longings for unconditional love and respect lay beneath the veneer of my life. Sadly, the result of denying and spiritualizing my brokenness caused me to become less human and humane. Misapplied biblical truths damaged my closest relationships and kept God from transforming me."

The radical transformation that has occurred in Fil's own life is what struck me most while reading *Breaking the Rules*. As I look back over the years of our friendship I'm dazzled by the diminishment of his restless striving to earn God's approval and his peaceful settling into a life of intimacy with God. With unspeakable gladness I give witness that what he declares is true: "Today my life offers proof that brokenness can be an instrument for positive change. Embracing my brokenness has allowed God's power to flow and thus transform my life."

People who are devoted to what Fil calls religion's "self-salvation blueprint" may feel that the freedom he espouses is too "un-rule-ly," too uncertain and too unrestricted for them to safely get on board. For those who insist that God never intended to include anyone and everyone, that we must be guided by rules and regulations, and that there are essential things that we must believe or do for God to love us, this book will not be their cup of tea.

On the other hand, for those who as Fil describes "have longed for the warm embrace of God only to get slapped down harshly by religion instead," this book will be like a refreshing breath of fresh air. Accepting the God of unrestricted love's invitation to trade his performance for intimacy, Fil Anderson has been ruined in a remarkable and delightful way. Convinced that rules are unnecessary when love guides our hearts, he's no longer able to tolerate religious distortions and misguided notions that render intimate fusion with God a just reward for our worthy performance. As St. Augustine said, "Love and do what you please."

If you plan on reading just one book this year on Jesus, this is the book that you must read. I suggest that the reader not just read this book, but pray over it page by page, as I have done.

Brennan Manning

Acknowledgments

Nearly three decades ago, Allan Emery wrote *A Turtle on a Fencepost: Little Lessons of Large Importance*. One of its bits of wisdom is, "If you ever see a turtle on a fencepost you can know that it didn't get there by itself." In other words, we don't accomplish anything in this world alone.

Writing a book illustrates the point. It simply doesn't happen without help. In my case, lots of help! The insights of many writers, teachers and friends are so integral to this book that, except for a few personal experiences I've included, the true author is the body of Christ. That notwithstanding, I'd like to especially thank several people.

Thank you, Kathy Helmers, for believing in my voice and urging me to use it when I write. You have been so much more than a literary agent. You have been a midwife and soulmate while remaining professional, direct, truthful and passionate about my message. Thank you for throwing caution to the wind and taking such a huge risk with me. I'll never be able to repay you.

Thank you, InterVarsity Press, for believing in me and my message enough to invest your exceptional reputation and resources into this book. Thank you especially for providing me with the outstanding assistance of Cindy Bunch. Thank you, Cindy, for walking beside me and helping me press ahead with my ideas until a book was born.

I am profoundly grateful for the people who support Journey Resources. Thank you for faithfully and generously partnering with me as I offer the message of God's love for all people everywhere: directing retreats, preaching and teaching, meeting with individuals who seek spiritual direction, writing, and walking alongside the poor, marginalized and disenfranchised of the world.

I'm indebted to a collection of brilliant literary companions who ignited my passion for breaking the rules and inspired me to begin trading performance for intimacy with God. Among them are Barbara Brown Taylor, Henri J. M. Nouwen, Mark Batterson, Richard Rohr, Joan Chittister, Tim Keller, Brian McLaren, Eugene Peterson, Philip Yancey, Joyce Rupp, Anselm Grün, Frederick Buechner, Gerald Sittser and Peter Gomes. While writing the final chapter I was especially grateful to Bruxy Cavey and Larry Crabb for the valuable insights and wisdom their respective books *The End of Religion* and *Soultalk* provided. Both assert that Jesus never intended to establish a new religion; instead his mission was to subvert the very idea of religion as a way to God, exposing it as Satan's hellish invention. Each offer a compelling portrayal of the world God originally intended and still desires, a world without religion.

Perhaps it's unnecessary for me to acknowledge Brennan Manning's unparalleled influence on my life. Yet I am compelled to do so. Countless times in his writing and preaching I've heard Brennan declare that love is the one criterion, the sole norm, the sign par excellence of authentic discipleship. For more than twenty years Brennan has embodied his message as he's loved me with disarming straightforwardness, uncommon tenderness and unrivaled kindness. Thank you, Brennan, for your investment in my life—you're a better friend than I deserve.

Thank you, Notorious Sinners (you know who you are), for rivaling all others in teaching me how to break the rules.

Thank you, Bill Yates, Jerry and Regina Clark, Vic Cochran, Mike Fowler, Marion McCollum, David Routh, Nigel Alston, Mal McSwain and especially Jerome Daley, for your demonstrations of uncommon patience and kindness as you read and reread my manuscript, graciously offering with candor your priceless editorial suggestions.

Thank you to those people, for whom my admiration is immense, who were willing to read my manuscript and offer their generous words of endorsement.

Thank you, Mike and Susie, Bill and Joann, Steve and Robin, and Johnny and Sue, for doing life together with Lucie and me. Thank you for offering us a place to shed our tears, express our disappointments, expose our failures and celebrate our joys.

Thank you, Vic and Susan Cochran, Bob and Ann Rodman, and Lynn and Ida Page, for providing me the perfect space in which to write and for your encouragement along the way.

It was after this book was in the copyeditor's hands that Paul Barclay suddenly died. We had been friends for three decades. If ever there was a religious bone in Paul's life, it had been broken. Paul was the most perfect embodiment of a rule breaker I have ever known. His intimate union with Jesus radiated to others God's love, humor and kindness.

I've been blessed with the greatest in-laws anyone could ever ask or pray for. Thank you, Ben and Enid Kennedy, for your love and support.

When I think of my mom and dad, I'm reminded of the lady to whose memory this book is dedicated. Like her, they did what they could. Thank you, Mom and Dad, for loving me through every stage of my life.

God declares, "A man's greatest treasure / is his wife— / she is a gift from the LORD" (Proverbs 18:22 CEV). Thank you, Lucie, for consistently being the most convincing proof I've witnessed that

God's Word is true. You are my greatest treasure, and each new day I love you more than the day before.

The three greatest treasures my life with Lucie has produced are our children. They are my heroes. Our daughter Meredith has one of the strongest yet most tender hearts I've ever known. I love you, Meredith, and I love Gabe, who sees you as his greatest treasure. Our son Will is bright and devoted to living his life fully with integrity. I admire his determination. I love you, Will, and I love Lauren, who is your greatest treasure. Our son Lee is wise beyond his years, and I marvel at his maturity, sense of justice and compassionate love for others, especially those on the fringes. I love you, Lee.

Above all, thank you, Jesus, for loving me beyond my wildest dreams and assuring me that I have all that it takes to be all that you have ever wanted me to be: your beloved Fil.

Introduction

Breaking the Rules

"As long as a relationship is ruled by love, the rule of law is obsolete."

ROBERT BILMONT

The handwriting in the front of my first Bible, the King James Version bound in black imitation leather, is unmistakably that of a child. I recognize it as my own. The inscription simply says: "Fil accepted Jesus Christ on February 26, 1961." Looking back, I'm still not sure what happened to me on that day.

I grew up in the South. Smack dab on the buckle of our nation's Bible belt. From early childhood I was taught that religion was the only ticket to the best life in this world. The North Carolina church I attended provided me with a tightly sealed view of God, the world and me. Since ours was the kind of family that showed up whenever the doors were opened, I lived within the pervasive cloud of the church's influence, which narrowed my vision and shaped the borders of my world. Growing up there, I learned about our corner on God's truth, and anyone who dared to disagree with us was either flirting with hell or already headed there.

My religion was characterized by a code of requirements, those activities or beliefs necessary to gain good standing with God. As I grew older, the essential truths associated with my religion became increasingly precise and the boundaries surrounding it more

constricting. Vigilantly, my religion taught me that God is powerful, flawless, and provoked to anger by my weakness, defects and
disregard.

In ironic contrast to the freedom it was alleged to provide,
religion enslaved me to a rigid and demanding regimen of rules.
This self-salvation blueprint became the pattern I was to follow
if I were to have any hope that God would recognize me as "fit
for heaven." Attend religious services. Show acts of generosity
and kindness (*show* being the operative word). Believe sound
doctrine. Avoid immoral activity. Read the Bible. Pray. Obey the
rules. Think pure thoughts. Boldly share the truth with others.
Don't cuss. Don't drink. Don't smoke. Carefully guard your appearance and reputation.

These telltale signs were regarded as the only means to acquir-
ing an abundant life and thereby guaranteeing security, acceptance, love and forgiveness. Since this was the life I wanted and
was striving for, I dedicated myself again and again to believing
and behaving properly. Yet, despite my desire and determined efforts, I rarely felt that I was making steady progress. Instead it
seemed that for every step forward, I took two steps back. The
only abundance I experienced was mounting feelings of disappointment.

I was ten years old in February 1961 when a traveling revival
preacher came to town. And he was mad! Mad at all the sinners
there—and mad at me. At least that's the way I remember it. The
first night of the revival I felt overpowering shame and regret as he
described our wickedness and the gory details of Jesus' death. Feeling as though he was speaking directly to me, I listened intently as
the preacher recited the latter half of a familiar verse, "While we
were still sinners, Christ died for us" (Romans 5:8 NIV). The dreadful climax came when he urged each of us, before going to sleep that
night, to seriously ask ourselves, "If I were to die and face God to-

night, how could I expect a holy God to allow me entrance into heaven? Why should God not cast me into hell's fiery furnace?"

It was a traumatic thing for a ten-year-old to go to bed feeling guilty, ashamed and afraid, especially when those feelings were provoked by the preaching of what was meant to be good news. Before drifting off to sleep, I remember telling God, "I'm sorry for being so bad."

What if, instead of attempting to scare the hell out of us (which has never been very effective with me), the preacher had emphasized the extravagant love and outrageous mercy of God?

What if, instead of stressing the magnitude of our depravity, he'd emphasized God's enormous goodness?

What if, when quoting that biblical passage, he'd included the preceding words of that verse, "God proves his love for us" (Romans 5:8 NRSV)?

What if, instead of intimidating us with the threat of torture, he'd approached us with the assurance of God's protection?

What if the "gospel" he preached had actually been good news?

Tragically, as a needy ten-year-old I didn't hear or see the good news in the religion that was offered. Instead of leading me to realize that I was God's beloved, he led me to believe that I was God's biggest disappointment.

AN INVITATION

How about you? Have you longed for the warm embrace of God, only to get slapped down harshly by religion? If so, this book is especially for you. Its message spells relief for tired and weary souls burned out by the demands and pressures that unbending rule-keeping religion requires. It will urge you to trade the rigors of religious performance for intimacy with Jesus, whose astonishing invitation is simply "Live in me. Make your home in me just as

I do in you" (John 15:4). Jesus' home is a place for everyone; it's a place of welcoming love, unconditional acceptance and endless assurances of affection.

I introduce an alternative path—the beauty of brokenness— using the Mark 14 story about the woman who captured Jesus' heart when she broke an expensive jar of perfume to anoint him. An uninvited dinner guest, this woman valued intimacy with Jesus over her reputation among the religious leaders of her day. When they leveled the charge that her gift was a waste, Jesus elevated its value by decreeing that it was a beautiful thing. Her life fused with his; she embodied what Jesus believed: If love guides our hearts, rules are unnecessary. Although Jesus never made breaking the rules a worthy goal in and of itself, he made clear the point that rule keeping is pointless if it's not an expression of something deeper. As we give up striving to fix ourselves, we find that the cracks in our fragmented lives become illuminated with the power of God's love, which shines into the lives of others. The women and men who are filled with light are those who have gazed deeply into the darkness of their own broken existence.

Jesus said, "I have come to call not those who think they are righteous, but those who know they are sinners" (Matthew 9:13 NLT). When we understand what he meant by this, we find the courage to confess our fears and insecurities, and plunge into the depths of God's love for us. *Breaking the Rules* invites you to quit trusting in your own ability to live for God, and simply trust in God instead.

Each chapter concludes with a few questions or ideas to ponder. Coming up with the right answer isn't the purpose. That's a "rule" we sometimes need to break. I hope they'll slow you down and encourage you to spend some time considering how you can trade performance for intimacy with God. After all, it's the home you've always longed for.

1 Is Your Faith in God or Religion?

"In the beginning the church was a fellowship of men and women
centering on the living Christ. Then the church moved to Greece where it
became a philosophy. Then it moved to Rome where it became an
institution. Next, it moved to Europe, where it became a culture. And,
finally, it moved to America where it became an enterprise."

RICHARD HALVERSON

During a week of revival meetings in February 1961, I
concluded that religion must provide the best answer to the question, What's the best way to live? So, on the evening of February
26, 1961, the final night of our church's revival services, I responded to the invitation for those "lost in sin to come forward
and commit your life to God." As people sang "Just as I Am," I
walked the aisle to lay my life on the altar. I knew from then on
that my eternal security would be determined by how well I con-
formed to my religion's rules and rituals.

So *religion* became the center of my life. It was a brilliantly designed and seductively attractive marketing program whereby life
with Jesus was reduced to doctrinal beliefs and moral command-
ments. Well-intentioned teachers, preachers and parents, who sincerely believed God had given them responsibility for training me,
delivered the program in carefully worded vision statements, mo-

tivational slogans and mission strategies.

Immediately I began learning my religion's vocabulary, memorizing its rules, and adopting its customs and practices. I swallowed it hook, line and sinker, while ignoring the cry of my soul for the kind of faith that makes life possible. Looking back I see that my religion had made itself God, demanding things that God abhors: division of people, diminishment of self and narrow closed-mindedness.

In the process I became "churched" rather than transformed. Systematically taught how to apply a cosmetic brand of godliness that was fear-based and that produced guilt and shame, I was folded into a homogeneous belonging system that resulted in conformity and expediency. It was little more than a permanent evasion of reality—a compromise with life. While conforming to an outward code of conduct, I and other members of my church offered one another an apparent justification for lives that were basically the same as our neighbors', whose perspectives were merely those of the world and its fleeting values.

Years later, I had become an accomplished religious professional—a relentless overachiever whose self-image was based on hard work and clean living. I earned love and approval by doing and performing. Religiously trained to define myself around the Herculean demands of roles and activities, my credo was: "If you want to be loved, make yourself lovable." My well-informed head knew about the unconditional love of God, but my ill-informed heart had no knowledge of it at all, only a desperate longing.

My religion's answer to, What's the best way to live? was essentially the same as Betty Crocker's answer to, What's the best way to successfully bake a scrumptious dessert? All religion requires of us is to gather the proper ingredients, carefully fold them into our life and then remain exposed to the proper amount of heat. Yet my life was haunted by the recognition that either my mix was flawed or I was half-baked. Despite my best efforts to get my life right, something always went wrong.

SHAME AND DESPAIR

Deep within I yearned for a more nurturing way of living than my religion provided. I longed for a reason to hope that God's goodness would make up for what was lacking in me. I craved being able to believe that when I was weak, God would be my strength. I wanted to know that when I felt abandoned, God would be with me. But more than anything, I ached with shame and despair, knowing that my life was not the way my religion prescribed. My life experience challenged all the absolutes religion had taught me. Religion had bound and gagged me. It had tied my soul down and nailed it to an endless list of rules and dogma.

In March of 1961, just a few weeks after "committing my life to follow and become like Christ," which is how they referred to a conversion in my church, I experienced my first major failure. I was playing basketball with friends when I spontaneously uttered a word that my religion labeled as clearly out-of-bounds. Time stood still for a moment, and then I rushed off the court with tears flooding my eyes. "What an idiot! I've blown it! What a miserable disappointment I am to God."

Soon I was back on course, vowing to try harder and never curse again. Those more experienced in these matters had taught me that God forgives those who are regretful, and that if I were wise I would see this as a lesson learned—that if I tried hard enough, it wouldn't have to be learned again.

Although religion had promised me the gift of freedom, the emphasis was increasingly on the essential achievement of my religion's demanding requirements. Despite my longing for assurance that I'd been forgiven by a loving and accepting God, I was never able to know for certain. It seemed that whenever I managed to gather "enough" right belief and behavior on the religious scale I'd do something stupid and wind up with too much weight on the opposite end, which undermined my confidence.

The tragic truth is: my religion lied to me. It lied when it told me that the best way to live was with rules, systems and formulas. It misled me when it reduced following Jesus to religion—a system where performance is substituted for faithful trusting, where rules take precedence over grace. It lied when it declared that being a Christian depended on me. It deceived me when it suggested that living in relationship with Jesus demanded that I become a better person. It failed when it didn't make clear that life with Jesus is more about him and less about me.

Religion introduced me to a pared-down god who was obligated to provide the things I yearned for as long as I held up my end of the bargain by conscientiously *believing* and *doing* the required things. This vision of God appealed to my desire to remain in control of my life. Like a "must have" consumer product, it promised to enable me to reach my potential, to help me gain others' admiration and respect, to develop my God-given gifts and talents, and to provide me with the life principles necessary for successful living.

The most lethal thing about my religion is that it offered assurance it did not provide. For that reason, as strange as it may seem, an atheist may have been in a safer position than me. At least the atheist would not have been living a lie, falsely believing he or she is in a relationship with God. The deadly mistake religion led me into was relying on it to give to me what it could not offer.

Thus I became a compulsive overachiever, an out-of-control work addict, what author Parker Palmer calls a "functional atheist." Although I spoke of God as being powerful and in control, my actions suggested that God either didn't exist or was critically ill. Religion forced me to live in the densely populated world of illusion, thinking that unless I was making it happen, nothing was happening. My life became malformed by an erroneous image of a too-small God and a too-big me. Once firmly planted, my mistaken views made arrogance second nature, and my life perilously spun out of control.

I now recall with delight an agonizing night, nearly twenty years ago, when I finally decided that I could no longer live this way. Although I had made a name for myself within the Young Life organization I served, I was physically exhausted and spiritually demoralized. My desperate striving to get my life right had been dogged since childhood by the haunting doubt that it would never happen, given the obvious (yet only to me) fact that I was hopelessly flawed. The result of the denial and displacement of my guilt and fear was shameless deceit, and it had led to the utter loss of integrity. I was fed up and disgusted with my fraudulent life and was determined to change. Once again, in a nearly broken down state, I asked God, "Have I ever really known you? Do I have a relationship with you, or is it simply religion that I have known?"

THE PROBLEM WITH RELIGION

Religion led me to live badly by teaching me to believe the wrong things and thus do the right things for the wrong reasons. The words Jesus spoke that were intended to keep this in focus are concise and clear: "I am the way, and the truth, and the life" (John 14:6 NRSV). However, we must do the Jesus *truth* in the Jesus *way* to get the Jesus *life*, and the problem with religion is that it makes this virtually impossible. Always yielding to what seems easier (and within our reach and control), religion stresses what we are to believe and do; then it urges us to rely on our own resources to accomplish it.

For years my allegiance was to good moral habits and churchy routines. Consequently, thinking that I was building a bridge to God, I instead erected a wall between myself and God and wound up living in the illusion that this constitutes a relationship with God. What I couldn't imagine is the truth that God's sole interest is our hearts, not our trivial expressions of reverence and respectability. What my religion prevented me from realizing is that God wants a relationship, and the only alliance that God enters into is one in which God is the total giver and we are the receiver.

The problem with religion is that it distorted my vision, leaving me with an amazing capacity for missing the point. Jesus explained the condition in these terms: "Though seeing, they do not see; / though hearing, they do not hear or understand" (Matthew 13:13 NIV). Jesus rolled out the cure when he unrolled the scroll and read the prophet's words:

> "The Spirit of the Lord is upon me,
>   because he has anointed me
>   to bring good news to the poor.
> He has sent me to proclaim release to the captives
>   and recovery of sight to the blind,
>   to let the oppressed go free." (Luke 4:18 NRSV)

Religion kept me from recognizing God's plain and simple intent:

> I want you to show love,
>   not offer sacrifices.
> I want you to know me
>   more than I want burnt offerings. (Hosea 6:6 NLT)

Religion prevented me from grasping this most essential truth: "Christ made a single sacrifice for sins, and that was it! . . . It was a perfect sacrifice by a perfect person to perfect some very imperfect people. By that single offering, he did everything that needed to be done for everyone" (Hebrews 10:11-14). Thus in a deaf, dumb and blind state I was determined to impress God and win favor by fixing myself. Yet eventually I was overwhelmed and defeated by the impossible challenge and wound up wallowing in guilt and shame, and sadly insulting the God I strove to please.

The problem with religion is that it saddles us with an impossible task: mending our own errant ways. Religion leads us to believe that on our own we can achieve a relationship with God by doing something impossible: keeping all the rules and being very, very good. Therefore, and tragically so, people who make an apparent success of the religious life are often in the gravest danger of missing out on the gift they are striving hopelessly to obtain. Especially when they make the horrendous mistake of thinking that God and religion are the same, and in the end make religion God.

SOMETHING ALTOGETHER DIFFERENT

An especially significant problem in our society is that in the minds of many people Christianity *is a religion*, and the only alternative to it (besides some other world religion) is being waywardly irreligious. And one of the surest signs that you might not recognize the unique and radical nature of Jesus' gospel is by arrogantly assuming that you do. Christianity isn't a religion; it's something altogether and completely different.

Religion is a human activity devoted to the impossible task of reconciling God to humanity and humanity to itself. Therefore when Jesus said, "Come to me. Get away with me and you'll recover your life. . . . Walk with me and work with me. . . . Keep company with me and you'll learn to live freely and lightly" (Matthew 11:28-30), we can rest assured that he wasn't inviting those striving to please God to be religious or irreligious, moral or immoral, conservative or liberal. Nor was he calling them to something in-between.

The gospel is the astonishing declaration that God's life-saving mission was accomplished before we were aware there was a problem. God has resolved the crisis without a whit of human assistance, leaving us in an extremely uncomfortable position: freedom guided by love in the context of God's radical insistence that we be our true selves.

Is it any wonder then that people devoted to religion are generally scared out of their wits and offended by Jesus while those on the outside of the closely guarded religious circle are intrigued and drawn to him? While on earth, Jesus consistently attracted the irreligious while insulting the Bible-believing, religious people. Some things never seem to change, do they?

THE ONE WHO KNOWS US

A poignant illustration of these contrasting reactions is seen in Jesus' encounter with a woman who came alone to draw water from a well (John 4:5-42). Although numerous stories are told of his befriending moral, racial, political, gender and youthful outsiders, she was an outsider three times over. In the first place, she was a Samaritan, which made her a half-breed and full-blown pagan as far as the religious elite were concerned.

She was also, of course, a woman. I heard about one group of religious men aptly known as "the bruised and bleeding Pharisees" because they closed their eyes when they saw a woman, even if it meant walking into a wall and breaking their noses. Who said being religious was easy?

So she was a racial and gender outsider, and was also a promiscuous woman, a moral outsider. Respectable women visited the well in the cool hours of the morning, where they visited and talked about the latest news. This woman was one of the people they talked about.

Imagine her surprise when she arrives at the well in the heat of the day and sees this strange man sitting beside it. When he lifts his head and asks her for a drink, it's apparent he's no half-breed, he's a Jew. She must have wondered what he was doing there. Had he lost his way? Had he lost his mind to be talking to her? More than anything, had he lost his *religion?* Despite being an outsider, she knew about the Jews' rules about what they could eat and drink, and whom they could speak to. She knew that he'd be breaking the law if she let him drink from her bucket.

A conversation ensues, and while it's hard to tell whether they're on the same page, the woman at least realizes that she wants what Jesus is offering her. When she asks Jesus to give her the water he's been speaking of, he tells her to fetch her husband. It's an abrupt change of subject, to which she must respond. She might have said, "Here we were having a nice conversation about religion. Now why'd you have to ruin it by getting personal?" She could have easily told a lie.

Instead, she faces him squarely and acknowledges, "I have no husband," and with that trace of truth from her, Jesus tells her the rest of the truth about herself. It's worth noting that Jesus doesn't withdraw. If anything, he gets closer. Shockingly, he still wants a drink from her, and he wants to give her one too. Yet the intimacy of their encounter seems to overwhelm her.

So she takes the conversation back to religion again, a subject that's far less personal and invasive. Who can blame her? If he knows about all her husbands, there may be no end to the list of things he knows about her. It's much safer to foster a religious debate about Samaritans and Jews.

But her plan fails. When she withdraws, he advances. When she steps out of the spotlight, he steps into it. He shuts off her every means of escape. If she's determined to show him less of herself, then he will show her more of himself. And the next thing you know, he reveals to her that he is the Messiah.

What an incredible moment of openness: this irreligious outsider and God's Messiah stand face to face with no sham or pre-

tense about who they truly are. Each facing the other in broad
daylight, while all the rules and traditions of religion that separate
them lose their power and fade into nothingness.

By telling the woman who she is, Jesus reveals to her who he is.
By validating her identity, he confirms his own, and that's how it
still happens. Jesus is the one in whose presence you know who
you really are. "The Messiah is the one . . . who crosses all boundaries, breaks all rules, drops all disguises," says Barbara Brown
Taylor, "speaking to you like someone you have known all your
life, bubbling up in your life like a well that needs no dipper, so
that you go back to face people you thought you could never face
again, speaking to them as boldly as he spoke to you. 'Come and
see a man who told me everything I have ever done.'"

The Vast Discrepancy

Reflecting on this stunning account and the vast discrepancy it
illuminates between what my religion emphasized and the things
Jesus declared has been life-altering. It has resulted in the most
spectacular and consequential shift in the trajectory of my life.

While religion had insisted on *telling* me precisely and with utter certainty what to know and believe about God, Jesus was intent on taking me by the hand and *showing* me the God who is
beyond characterization, definition or comprehension. He used an
assortment of resources to set this process in motion, particularly
the influence and friendship of others, prayerful Bible reading,
and personal and directed retreats into solitude and silence.

The first and most essential thing Jesus was intent on reshap-
ing was my twisted and deformed view of God. For years I'd been
familiar with the story recorded in Luke 15 about a father and
his two sons. Typically referred to as the parable of the prodigal
son (perhaps projecting a bit), I'd always seen the rebellious son
as the central figure and identified with his rambunctious, dis-

graceful and disappointing journey.

I owe a particular debt of gratitude to Henri Nouwen and Timothy Keller, whose insights deepened and expanded my understanding of its implications. Both authors helped me recognize that it's shortsighted to take a story that begins "a man had *two* sons" and single out only one of the three characters as the sole focus. The story is as much about the elder brother as the younger, and as much about the father as the sons. And what Jesus says about the father is one of the most important truths revealed in the Bible.

The foundation of my understanding began to shift when I understood that *prodigal* doesn't mean "wayward" but "recklessly spendthrift." A prodigal is one who spends until they have nothing left to spend.

Thus *prodigal* is appropriate for describing the father in the story and his younger son. The father's welcome home was literally reckless, because he refused to hold his son's offenses against him or demand repayment. This timeless story portrays a radically different picture of God from the one religion presented to me! Jesus shows us the God of endless spending, who is nothing if not prodigal toward us. Jesus is the embodiment of this God.

Understanding this difference has altered the course of my life. To me there is now no greater statement about God in the Bible than this: "When he was still a long way off, his father saw him. His heart pounding, he ran out, embraced him, and kissed him" (Luke 15:20). Before the son could begin reciting his carefully crafted apology and plea for forgiveness, his father, without a trace of anger or resentment, but overcome with the emotion that unconditional love provokes, began lavishing him with unbridled affection and acceptance.

On another occasion, in what is referred to as the Beatitudes, Jesus clearly and succinctly declared God's economy of values. The Beatitudes portray the character of God's daughters and sons.

These are the ethics of God's people. With the Beatitudes, Jesus contradicted the religious system and made clear that the kingdom of God is the government of God in a person's life. It is the quiet, inner control center of our life and conduct nurtured by Christ who lives within our heart. In the Beatitudes Jesus intended to erase all doubt and confusion, making clear that only those whose lives reflect these values are his followers:

- *the poor in spirit*, who feel accepted by God and understand their reliance on God for everything
- *those who mourn*, who know and express their feelings, grieving the nature and effect of sin in themselves and in others
- *the meek*, who know they don't have to have it all together and have thus yielded control of their life to God and can be gentle with other people and themselves
- *those who crave uprightness*, who are more excited about God's agenda for themselves and the world than any other thing
- *those who are hurting, lonely or distressed* and, without dragging their feet, give unqualified aid
- *the pure in heart*, who don't pretend to be what they are not but are completely open and honest with God and others
- *the peacemakers*, who show people how to cooperate instead of compete or fight and how to discover their place in God's family
- *those who are persecuted because of their uprightness*, who stand with God and are willing to endure any difficult consequences

The contrast between the things Jesus said God cares about and what I was taught to value is startling. Religion trained me to believe that I must be disciplined, headstrong and independent, proud of my achievements, bold, full of virtue, discerning in distribution of mercy, always appearing to be good, regardless of my inner disposition, and radical in devotion to my religious beliefs and actions.

Truthfully, I might still be willing to accept these terms if my religious striving had produced a reasonable hope that it was capable of delivering the "goods" I'd been striving to acquire. But all religious striving ever earned for me was a hard-of-hearing heart and a life of restless longing and drowsy disappointment. Religion led me to become a man driven by guilt, while still clinging to the hope that my performance might gain God's acceptance. I was obsessed with and driven by determination to achieve enough goodness in order to make up for all of my badness. Yet as time wore on, the desperate longing to get my life right was relentlessly dogged by the nagging fear that it would never happen, given the obvious fact that I was hopelessly flawed.

After years of being ripped apart by the competing demands of my life as a religious professional, the cheese was sliding off my cracker. My lifestyle had made me sick. I had been deluded about myself for so long that dishonesty was not only acceptable but a necessary way of life. I knew that either a breakdown or a breakthrough was imminent.

When I got to the end of my rope, I decided to finally let go and landed in a safe, secluded retreat setting. There I opened my Bible and read about the death of Lazarus and how Jesus "cried with a loud voice, 'Lazarus, come out!' The dead man came out, his hands and feet bound with strips of cloth, and his face wrapped in a cloth. Jesus said to them, 'Unbind him, and let him go'" (John 11:43-44 NRSV).

The image touched me in a profound way and led me to wonder if the raising of Lazarus was a metaphor of what needed to happen inside me. Was it time for me to come out of the tomb my religion had imprisoned me in? Was Jesus about to instruct someone to "take off the grave clothes" that had kept me bound?

Called to follow Jesus, I had nonetheless resisted getting too close. Bound by guilt, shame and bitter disappointment, I was thus trapped in the erroneous belief that God could not love me. How could God possibly look at me without disgust? On the horns of this dilemma I knew there would be no wholeness until I was somehow able to enter into the fierce tenderness of God's love.

On the final morning of the retreat my spiritual director set my emancipation into motion. "Fil, you will never be free until you've named the things that hold you captive. Next you must allow God's definition of you to become your own definition of you. Fil, God is crazy about you! You are God's beloved. From this moment forward, that truth must become the most important truth that you know about yourself." Those prophetic words have since become the sacred hinge for my life. As the shame, guilt and disappointment that had constricted my soul began to lose its hold on me, I was ushered into a new way of being and of relating to God. I began to learn to recognize God's presence within and experience myself loved beyond reason.

Since then the truth that I'm God's beloved has been settling down slowly into my heart, and it's changing everything about my life, from the inside out. After years of desperate striving to be religious, finally, I'm throwing in the towel. Like some bogus product sold by a fly-by-night salesman, religion has failed to deliver what it promised. Like a poorly designed and shabbily constructed bridge, my religion became suspect and eventually I concluded that it could not deliver me to God's intended destination. Instead of providing me clear and unconditional access to God, it stood in the way, always with an outstretched hand, demanding some additional form of payment in order to advance.

LOSING MY RELIGION

Perhaps this explains why "losing my religion" has become my, and countless others', highest hope and deepest longing. Religion trained us to become experts in hiding, denying, pretending, eluding, averting, covering and avoiding the person we really are. Yet, to see who we are meant to be, who we are capable of being if we will stop running and start looking, is what following Jesus is all about. Tragically, knowing and becoming ourselves is not allowed within the context of religion's rules and rituals.

In dramatic fashion my life (past and present) is a mirror reflection of Aladdin's life. No. Not the subject in a story in the *Arabian Nights*. Not the one with the magic lamp. I'm talking about a dog whose story I read in the sports section of a bogus online newspaper. The headline read: "Greyhound Bitterly Disappointed After Finally Catching Mechanical Rabbit." The journalist covering the story reported that "Aladdin," a greyhound who had spent years racing at the Jacksonville Dog Track in Jacksonville, Florida, had become devastated by the outcome, when he finally succeeded in catching the rabbit, only to discover that it was not real.

"Boy do I feel stupid" was the first comment Aladdin offered reporters. "I feel like such a fool. I've wasted my life chasing around this . . . mechanical rabbit. I became obsessed with it. . . . [B]ut that rabbit represented something to me. And now, to find out it wasn't even a real rabbit, well it's just devastating."

One might wonder: "What's a dog to do after the truth has been revealed?" but for Aladdin the answer was certain.

"I'm not going to keep chasing plastic bunnies for the rest of my life. There are real bunnies out there, waiting to be eaten. . . . It's time I started to live a little."

Trust me. I understand Aladdin's despair and determination. The appalling realization that religion, which had provided a way of expressing my belief in God, was nonetheless incapable of providing me a transformed life was devastating.

Aladdin and I lived parallel lives. We were both driven to chase what our hearts were set on catching. We both performed before a shouting crowd, some of whom were personally invested in the outcome of our race. His supporters were self-absorbed gamblers who laid down bets with high hopes of financial gain, while mine were parents, teachers, preachers, relatives and friends with the noblest of intentions who pointed me in the right direction and were hoping that I would remain on the "straight and narrow."

Our idle moments were often spent dreaming of the day when we sank our teeth into the prize. However, the prize eventually proved fraudulent. Even the crowd's approval, which we also enjoyed, proved to be less than enough to satisfy our deepest longing. Yet the pats on our heads and the "you're a good boy" remarks were enough to keep us going.

Today, just like Aladdin, I'm discovering that there's a far better way to live. Like him, I'm realizing that what I've always longed for actually exists. There is a more nurturing way to live than my religion provided—from my heart. Yet, it's not as neatly arranged or as clearly marked as a circular racetrack; neither can I trust the crowd's response to determine whether I'm performing well. While it's not safe and predictable, it is a life worth living.

AN EXTRAORDINARY LIFE

Knowing me and understanding what makes me tick better than I ever will, God was aware that I'd never discover a more nurturing way to live until I had a clear picture of how living that way appears. Loving me more than I ever will comprehend, God arranged for a person to come crashing into my life at just the right time: Mike Yaconelli.

From the moment we first met in 1988 until our last moment together, Mike's lifestyle provoked me to reevaluate how I was living. Mike was unlike any man I had ever encountered. To be honest, I didn't always enjoy being with him. Sometimes Mike scared me. There were times when he intimidated me. I often felt an awkward and restless dis-ease when we were together. By the time we met, Mike had been living from deep within his heart long enough to recognize me as someone who had lived most of his life as an imposter. Mike saw the meaning hidden behind the image I often presented—and he called my bluff.

Mike and I had our first significant encounter a few years later while retreating with a group of men on the Mississippi coast. We were assigned to stay in a room together. I'd gotten up early on the first morning of the retreat and joined the others in our group for breakfast. Since Mike never showed up for breakfast, I returned to the room to check on him before our morning session began. Opening the door, I found him sitting on the side of his bed. He was bent forward with his head in his hands. Suddenly, with his hair a wild mess, he squinted at me and said, "You know, I've always been told that it takes a crook to catch a crook. Anderson, I've already got you pegged. You and I are much more alike than it appears. The only difference is this: I've quit trying to look like my life's all put together, but you're still desperately trying." Then with a tender smile, he added, "Fil, I'm looking forward to knowing the real you."

Mike's effect on me was like a defibrillator on an all-but-dead heart. When we first met my heart was shut down, but his seemed wide open, never more so than when he shared his heart with God. Mike was convinced that anything he held back from Jesus would end up hurting him. For that reason he appeared fearless and free to tell Jesus everything. There was never any editing in his relationship with Jesus. I especially cherish the memory of those stunning times when unflinchingly he revealed the darkness of his heart, asking Jesus to shine his light inside its shadowy recesses.

Mike's was a prophetic voice, unconventionally and bravely

challenging misguided followers of Jesus like me, and the church
throughout the world, to examine my relationship with Jesus in
an open and candid way. Unlike the experience of many, in Mike's
life God wasn't far off somewhere controlling the universe but always nearer to him than his next breath. Deep within his quick-
ened heart was the assurance that there was *never anything* in
God's heart but love for him.

As well as anyone I've known, Mike understood the difference
between religion and an authentic life with God. He also understood the difference between religious institutions and an authentic faith community. As the pastor of what he referred to as "the
slowest growing church in America," he affirmed the need of Jesus' followers to be linked with a faith community equipped to
teach and remind us of the things we believe and why we believe
them.

Without a doubt, God has persisted in teaching me a wildly different life with him. It routinely turns upside down and inside out
the values, training and conditioning that got me into trouble in
the first place. Finally, I'm discovering a more nurturing way to
live than religion could provide. At last, I'm learning how to live
from my *heart* instead of from my *head*.

PAUSE AND PONDER

- What's your view of God? Have you ever longed for God's warm
  embrace only to get slapped down harshly by religion instead?

- How about your view of yourself? Do you live more from your
  head or your heart?

2 The Myth That Jesus Thinks Like Us

"Religion has tended to create people who think they have God in their pockets, people with quick, easy, glib answers."

RICHARD ROHR

During the last few years of the twentieth century countless people purchased pens, pencils, bracelets, bangles, necklaces, T-shirts, caps, travel mugs, lunch bags and cutesy knickknacks emblazoned with the WWJD? logo. For twenty dollars we could buy the "What Would Jesus Do?" game, which was designed to challenge us to look at the role of Jesus in our life through thought-provoking questions. Each question dealt with life's everyday dilemmas and provided answers on how we might respond to them. Would we take the easy route in these situations or ask the ultimate question, What would Jesus do? For those who wished to have a ready reminder, there were WWJD? tattoos. Sadly, being a follower of Jesus had once again been reduced to something far less remarkable than it truly is.

Therein lies perhaps the most tragic characteristic of Christian religion. As an "outsider" from Mississippi bluntly observed in *unChristian*, "Christianity has become bloated with blind followers who would rather repeat slogans than actually feel true compassion and care. Christianity has become marketed and streamlined into a juggernaut of fear mongering that has lost its own heart." I sincerely believe that institutional, religious Christianity has probably done more to hinder the ideals of Jesus than any other agency in the world.

As I consider the professing Christians that I know, I see some whose lives have been made incomparably better by their faith and some made incomparably worse. Without a doubt, for every tenderhearted, gracious, forgiving person that I know, I can think of hardhearted, thoughtless, judgmental ones, and each of them claims to be a follower of Jesus. Those who work at their relationship with God most conscientiously and assert the most certainty about their faith are sometimes the least winsome. Like many of the religious folks that Jesus encountered, they get caught trying to be the gatekeepers of truth and wind up being self-righteous rather than genuinely righteous.

When our daughter Meredith worked in a restaurant, Sundays were her least favorite workdays because of the rude crowd who arrived after attending church. Resolving the conflict between the ideals Jesus established and the actual ways that religious Christians live—the way I often live—is an enormous and necessary challenge.

BEFORE THE FAD

Long before WWJD? became a profitable fashion fad, thirty-five church youth group members in Holland, Michigan, proposed to make the question a central part of their lives. They pledged to their youth leader and each other that for thirty days they would ask *What would Jesus do?* before every decision. Their inspirations were the characters in Charles Sheldon's century-old classic *In His Steps*, where the question first appeared. The book, often referred to by the youth group's leader as a favorite since her childhood, recounts the story of some ordinary church people solemnly vowing to act as Jesus would.

Wisely concerned that they would not actually remember to evoke the question, their leader began searching for something that would serve as a helpful reminder. She approached a member of the church who worked for a corporation that specialized in branding products with corporate logos or names. She gave WWJD? bracelets to her excited students, urging them to wear them at all times during the thirty-day challenge.

Neither she nor any of her youth group had imagined how much money a swarm of entrepreneurs and corporations would pocket off her innocent inspiration. But she does now. Estimates about how many bracelets have been sold in the United States range from fifteen million to fifty-two million. Even the Italian fashion designer Giorgio Armani and the National Basketball Association got in on the action, both of whom ordered thousands of text-imprinted bracelets.

Therefore, I was not surprised when the question was subjected to mockery and satire, giving rise to similar questions such as "Who Wants Jelly Donuts?" "Who would Jesus bomb?" "Would Jesus drive a Lexus, a Humvee or a fuel-efficient model car?" "What neighborhood would Jesus live in?" "Who would Jesus execute?" "Who would Jesus refuse health care?" "What country club would Jesus join?" and "Would Jesus vote for Republicans or Democrats or would he not vote?"

Presumably, the answer to the question WWJD? or, for that matter, any of the variations people contrived, is to be determined on the basis of Jesus' words and actions found in the Bible. Yet this is precisely where my consternation lies. An honest assessment of the past and current trends reveals that our answers often are determined by the beliefs and preferences of the person asking the question. Followers of religion always possess a personal agenda, ranging from liberal to conservative, and naturally assume that

Jesus would think or behave as they do, that he would reflect their own prejudices and practices. And if we're honest, we must admit that followers of religion have often gotten the answer wrong, at times horribly wrong.

The capacity that followers of religion claiming to be followers of Jesus have demonstrated for being wrong in their thinking and thus in their actions is reprehensible, shameful and unconscionable. I take no pleasure in calling this reality into the light, yet I stand in solidarity with Frederick Douglass, an American abolitionist, author, statesman and slave, who said, "I prefer to be true to myself, even at the hazard of incurring the ridicule of others, rather than to be false, and incur my own abhorrence." In his eloquent yet excruciating accounts, Douglass characterizes how "Christian religion" in the South was a mere façade behind which the most horrific crimes, appalling barbarity and hateful hypocrisy imaginable occurred. He asserted that being the slave of a religious master was the greatest calamity of all.

We need to carefully ponder his scathing indictment.

> Between the Christianity of this land, and the Christianity of Christ, I recognize the widest possible difference—so wide, that to receive the one as good, pure, and holy, is of necessity to reject the other as bad, corrupt, and wicked. To be the friend of the one is of necessity to be the enemy of the other. I love the pure, peaceable, and impartial Christianity of Christ: I therefore hate the corrupt, slaveholding, women-whipping, cradle-plundering, partial and hypocritical Christianity of this land. Indeed, I can see no reason, but the most deceitful one, for calling the religion of this land Christianity. I look upon it as the climax of misnomers, the boldest of all frauds, and the grossest of all libels.

I was born in the eastern section of North Carolina in February

1951. That was three years before the Supreme Court ruled in favor of integrated public schools. It was thirteen years before federal civil rights laws forced restaurants and motels to serve all races of people, and fourteen years before the U.S. Congress assured minorities of their right to vote in public elections. Meanwhile, the Ku Klux Klan, a domestic, secret terrorist organization, had a formidable presence where I lived.

I remember water fountains and public restrooms labeled with signs for "whites" and "coloreds." I recall segregated bus-station waiting areas and "colored" people walking past me on their way to the back of the bus one summer when I traveled to visit my grandparents. I can still remember the toilet sitting in the open part of a dimly lit room in my grandparents' basement. When I asked my grandparents why it was there they explained it was for the "n— woman" who cleaned their house and prepared their meals.

I remember my church's emphasis on delivering the message of God's unconditional love to all people. Yet I also remember heated debates about whether we would allow a "colored" person to join our church. Although the threat never materialized, I recall wondering why a "colored" person would want to join such a church.

Looking back today on these shameful memories, I realize that this might be the best opportunity I'll ever have to express the most heartfelt thing I might ever say. Therefore, I want to confess my shame, sorrow and regret for being so despicably wrong. It's taken a lot of years for God to break the dreadful iron grip of blatant racism on me—and sadly, I'm still held by some of its more subtle forms.

To illustrate more specifically how misguided I was without knowing it, there was a time when I detested the life of Dr. Martin Luther King Jr. and believed the hateful remarks I heard religious people make about him. Today I cannot dismiss or deny the distinctive centrality of his Christian conviction and the influence of this noble man whose dream of freedom was large enough to include a hateful racist like me.

None of the victories he won came effortlessly, and most didn't come during his lifetime. In an exchange between Dr. King and his colleague Roy Wilkins, who was angrily challenging his methods, I'm told Wilkins asked, "Martin, if you've desegregated anything by your efforts, kindly enlighten me."

"Well," Dr. King replied, "I guess about the only thing I've desegregated so far is a few human hearts." Dr. Martin Luther King Jr. knew Jesus well enough to know that the ultimate victory had to be won in people's hearts. As the possessor of one of those slow but sure-to-be-changed hearts, I'd have to agree.

Dr. King lived and died with a holy, God-given vision for reconciliation, redemption and the establishment of a new community. And he set this vision into motion, even in the heart of a racist bigot like me.

ARROGANT PRESUMPTION

The fatal characteristic of people devoted to religion is arrogant presumption regarding what God is going to do next and how God is going to do it. For instance, after God disclosed plans to harden Pharaoh's heart, Moses envisioned the immediate release of the Israelites, making him a national hero. However, when Pharaoh increased their hardship rather than allowing the Hebrews to leave, Moses' dream was shattered. Rather than becoming their hero, he became a scoundrel. Understandably, Moses returned to God and complained, "My Master, why are you treating this people so badly? And why did you ever send me? From the moment I came to Pharaoh to speak in your name, things have only gotten worse for this people. And rescue? Does this look like rescue to you?" (Exodus 5:22-23).

Truthfully, today I'm less confident to claim that I know for certain what Jesus would do in certain situations than I've ever been.

Jesus is mysterious and unpredictable. For that reason Jesus constantly censured the religious establishment: "For the sake of your tradition, you make void the word of God. You hypocrites! Isaiah prophesied rightly about you when he said: 'This people honors me with their lips, but their hearts are far from me; in vain do they worship me, teaching human precepts as doctrines'" (Matthew 15:6-9 NRSV). Jesus was continually deconstructing the prevailing views that the religious clung to, as well as their expectations about what the Messiah would accomplish.

Much of the disappointment that religious devotees experience is not the result of God's failure to do the things promised. Instead, it comes from false and arrogant assumptions about how God should and will act. Often the disappointment is exacerbated because personal preferences and desires have been added to the equation. Thus we wind up confused about how to live, and we despair when things don't turn out as we presumed they should.

Jesus was in constant conflict with the religious establishment in his day (and today) because he embodied a God who is radically different from what they expected or desired. Jesus turned upside down and inside out their presumptuous vision of God's values, character and personality. Thus having expected to be principal players in God's kingdom, they were appalled when they found themselves without any part. Meanwhile the irreligious misfits were dazzled and delighted by Jesus' winsome manifestation of God, and shocked when Jesus called them brothers and sisters and friends.

Often Jesus used the power of story to illustrate the shocking truth about God. The parable about the prodigal son portrays the destructive selfishness of the younger son but also criticizes the elder son's moralistic life. There's something in the story to challenge everyone's categories as Jesus declares that both sons are alienated from God. Jesus told it to bring restoration, a revolution in the way religious people viewed God. He told it to set free those enslaved to list-heeding, rule-keeping religion. It is a sincere call to break free.

I imagine Jesus may have fought back tears as he told this story because some of the people listening thought they had God in their pockets. It's just as easy to imagine the religious people growing hot beneath their collars. After all, they had God pegged, certain that God's keeping a list and checking it twice to find out who is naughty or nice.

Meanwhile they thought that people unlike them, those who were irreligious and lousy at obeying religious rules, didn't have a snow cone's chance in hell of being loved and accepted by God. Obviously, *they* didn't pass the test. They'd done nothing to qualify for God's favor. But instead of a bookkeeping, list-checking, nit-picking legalist, Jesus confronted them with a God who runs to embrace pathetic failures. It's a theological curve ball of epic proportions. Instead of a God who's predictably quick to judge, Jesus' God is unpredictably gracious and forgiving, like a kind and loving parent, yet much more.

Most conspicuous is the fact that there is no list-keeping in this God's heart. There's not a single religious requirement that must first be met for forgiveness to be granted. In fact, there's not any mention of forgiveness, let alone any earning of it, because forgiveness is already taken care of. It is, as Jesus said, "finished" (John 19:30 NRSV).

Those who were shocked by the apparent disparity in the story Jesus told had no basis for reacting that way. Centuries before, God had inspired the prophet Isaiah to clarify the reason for the presumed disparity, and certainly they would have been familiar with the truth about the God it conveyed: "I don't think the way you think. / The way you work isn't the way I work. . . . / For as the sky soars high above earth, / so the way I work surpasses the way you work, / and the way I think is beyond the way you think" (Isaiah 55:8-9). Several centuries later, Jesus appeared as "the visible expression of the invisible God" (Colossians 1:15 Phillips) and became the clearest picture of God we could ever see—if only we would see.

JESUS' MADDENING UNPREDICTABILITY

The particular difficulty that religious people have often encountered in their dealings with Jesus is his maddening *unpredictability*. He's simply impossible to control! He breaks all social etiquette in relating to people. He acknowledges no barriers or human divisions. There is no category of sinners he isolates himself from. Simply stated, Jesus is a miserable failure at meeting religious people's expectations of him. He connects with the kinds of people he should disregard. He attends the wrong dinner parties. He is rude to respected religious leaders and polite to whores. He reprimands his own followers and praises outsiders and riffraff. "All in all," writes Barbara Brown Taylor, "this is not a man you want teaching the first-grade Sunday school class (although he is crazy about children)."

Jesus continuously criticized the religious establishment for imagining that they had solved the eternal mystery that he embodied. He persistently deconstructed the prevailing views of the religious authorities regarding the will of God, as well as their expectation about what the Messiah was to accomplish and how it was to be completed. His words and actions were as whimsical and inscrutable as God's in the Old Testament, and they often contradicted the values of his followers.

Meanwhile, I routinely encounter people who arrogantly believe they are right in their beliefs about God, theology, heaven and hell, and who is going where, not to mention sexuality, morality, global issues, politics, abortion and a plethora of other things.

They are also arrogantly certain that people who disagree with them or question their certainty are not Jesus' followers.

Also I regularly meet people who seem repulsed by people claiming to be followers of Jesus, viewing them with suspicion and doubt, often referring to them as Bible-thumping, law-keeping, people-alienating, tradition-worshiping, fast-talking, never-listening fundamentalist bullies who carelessly give too-easy answers for life's darkest and deepest ills. Some say that even if the arrogantly certain crowd were proved right, they wouldn't want to be like them because they're so unlike Jesus.

I'm genuinely concerned for both groups, having belonged to either one at various stages in my life. To their credit both sides mostly agree it's important that we have convictions and follow our conscience. Thus my plea is to remember that not one of us has ever seen what is in the heart of another person. No one has ever seen a motive, not even one of our own motives. Therefore none of us is in a position to judge well what is in another person's heart. As a friend of mine is fond of saying, "Blaming and judging, I've judged is no blamed good."

To my brothers and sisters who are followers of Jesus I'd like to extend humbly (hoping you'll remember that it takes a crook to catch one) an additional appeal. I don't believe that "certainty" is the enemy. I believe the enemy is "arrogance." The prophet Micah delivered one of the most memorable statements in the Old Testament defining a right relationship with God.

> He has shown you, O man, what is good.
>   And what does the LORD require of you?
> To act justly and to love mercy
>   and to walk humbly with your God. (Micah 6:8 NIV)

Micah here summarized the major themes of his nearest contemporaries. "But let justice roll on like a river, / righteousness like a never-failing stream!" (Amos 5:24 NIV). "For I desire mercy, not sacrifice, / and acknowledgment of God rather than burnt offerings" (Hosea 6:6 NIV). "Once more the humble will rejoice in the LORD; / the needy will rejoice in the Holy One of Israel" (Isaiah 29:19 NIV).

Recently I visited with a grief-stricken friend. There was not a trace of arrogant certainty in the room. A few months earlier he and his wife had buried their two-year-old son, who had fought a long and painful battle with leukemia.

"I don't know how to pray anymore," he confessed. "How do I pray to a God who anticipates an avalanche of medical bills that I can't see coming and makes resources available that I never asked God to provide? How do I pray to a God who holds onto me when I'm falling apart, who guides me when I'm lost and afraid and too broken to ask for help? How do I pray to a God whom I've been assured is faithful and kind yet refuses to spare the life of my two-year-old son when that's the only thing I begged God to do?"

Truthfully it's easy for me to understand why we prefer living in the illusion of a predictable god. Especially in light of the unpredictable world we live in today. Particularly since September 11, 2001, our world has radically altered. More than ever before, we're gripped by unpredictability and uncertainty. Of course, the safety that we arrogantly counted on and previously enjoyed was always an illusion. Nonetheless, it was a comforting illusion that allowed us to imagine we were safely in control.

I believe those of us who are followers of Jesus will live our lives more authentically and confess our faith with greater integrity when we openly confess our uncertainty. Yet sadly, those who are devoted to religion are granted no such freedom. Flannery O'Connor was speaking prophetically when she declared, with characteristic tartness, that we shouldn't expect faith to clear everything up for us. After all, we're pilgrim people, that's why we're following Jesus, and when we finally get our spiritual house in order, we'll be dead. That's what following Jesus, O'Connor believed, consists of and how it works. We live with enough certainty about the essential elements of our faith to be able to make our way, but it's often in darkness. "Faith is about trust, not certainty," she advised. "Don't expect faith to clear things up for you. It is trust, not certainty."

IN THE BEGINNING

If we don't wish to believe the myth that Jesus thinks just like us, the best place to begin is in the beginning. Who could have foreseen that God would bring about his Son's birth in such a dark and difficult fashion? How outrageous and unpredictable it is that he, who would be slaughtered by men acting like animals, was born among animals. Who would have predicted that Jesus, who called himself "the living bread that came down from heaven" (John 6:51 NIV), would get his start in a place where animals eat?

Much like Elijah's encounter on the mountain when God came in the "thin silence," the God who came to this earth did not come in a raging whirlwind or in a consuming fire. "Unimaginably," Philip Yancey writes, "the Maker of all things shrank down, down, down, so small as to become an ovum, a single fertilized egg, barely visible to the naked eye, an egg that would divide and redivide until the fetus took shape, enlarging cell by cell inside a nervous teenager." He "emptied himself, / taking the form of a slave / . . . And . . . / he humbled himself / and became obedient to the point of death" (Philippians 2:7-8 NRSV). How outrageously unpredictable is his story!

In humble contrast to the royal treatment some religious people anticipated, God's unpredictable walk through our neighborhood took place when "there was no room in the inn, but there was room in the stable." The inn was a crossroad of public opinion and a rallying place of the high and the mighty. But the stable was a place for the outcasts, the ignored and the forgotten. The world might have expected the Son of God to be born, if he was to be born at all, in a royal setting. A stable would be the last place where one would expect him to be born. The possible lesson for those asking WWJD?: *God often appears in the most unpredictable places.*

To people who partitioned off a separate chamber for God in the temple and wouldn't dare to pronounce or even spell out his name, God made an unpredictable visit as a baby in a feeding trough. What could have been less predictable than a newborn infant wrapped in a blanket, relying on an ill-equipped teenager to provide his next meal? In Jesus, God offered the most humble and approachable way of relating to us, one that did not involve any degree of fear. The possible lesson for those asking WWJD?: *God often appears in the most unpredictable places.*

No one in their right mind would have predicted that the One who clothed the fields with grass and flowers would himself be naked, that the Alpha and the Omega would have such a pathetic beginning and meet with such a tragic end, that he who formed the world with his hands would have the weak and tiny hands of an infant, that the living Word would start out cooing, that he who would become the Savior of the world would have to escape the genocide of a hateful and merciless king. Perhaps the lesson for those asking WWJD? is that *God often appears in the most unpredictable places.*

The term *loser* is a crude word often used in reference to someone who's disadvantaged, down-and-out or underprivileged, and is therefore viewed by others as a dud, failure or dork. Yet I cannot help but conclude that though the world may be tilted toward the successful, wealthy and powerful, God is tilted toward "losers." Consider God's portrayal of how Jesus would appear and be received when he came to earth. God said to be on the lookout for "a

scrawny seedling, / a scrubby plant in a parched field." God gave
advance notice that there'd be "nothing attractive about him, /
nothing to cause us to take a second look." Therefore we could
expect him to be "looked down on and passed over" (see Isaiah
53:2). God didn't mince words when giving the bleak forecast: One
look at Jesus and people would turn away. They'd look down on
him, thinking he was scum (see Isaiah 53). Nonetheless, "He has
brought down rulers from their thrones but has lifted up the humble," said Mary in the Magnificat. "He has brought down the powerful from their thrones, / and lifted up the lowly; / he has filled
the hungry with good things, / and sent the rich away empty"
(Luke 1:52-53 NRSV).

Clearly Jesus' sensibilities were affected most profoundly by the
poor, the powerless and the oppressed—in short, the losers of his
day. Ever since then biblical scholars have debated whether God
has a preference for the poor. Nonetheless, it is an indisputable
fact that God alone arranged the circumstances in which to be
born on earth—without power or wealth, without justice or rights.
Thus God's preferential choices speak for themselves.

Nothing in human history could have unfolded in a more
shocking and unpredictable fashion than Jesus' entrance into his
own world through the back door, an entry typically reserved for
servants. What raw courage it required for God to set aside all
rightful advantages and take his place on an equal plane among
those he created only to be met with arrogance, contempt, skepti-
cism and disregard.

If knowing what to expect was a puzzle at Jesus' birth, who
could have predicted the surprises his preteen years would provide? On the first Passover after Jesus' twelfth birthday, his parents took him to Jerusalem. After the ceremonial rites were completed, the men and women of Nazareth left in separate caravans
to meet again at night. It would be natural to assume that Jesus

would be in their company. However, a day later when they were unable to locate him among their relatives and friends, there must have been an overwhelming wave of panic.

With Jesus nowhere to be found, Mary and Joseph did the obvious thing and returned to Jerusalem in search of him. Try imagining this: "After three days." Ouch! Three days is a long, long time, especially when your son (who also happens to be the Messiah) is missing! Finally, consider the indescribable joy and relief they must have felt when they found him in the temple courts, sitting among the teachers, listening and asking questions. After Mary's agitated question about why he had treated his parents so thoughtlessly, the only predictable response is apologetic. However, Jesus' explanation was outrageously inconsiderate, "'Why were you searching for me? Did you not know that I must be in my Father's house?' But they did not understand what he said to them" (Luke 2:49-50 NRSV). For crying out loud! Who could blame them for not understanding? That is, until you look a bit more closely.

LOOKING IN THE UNPREDICTABLE PLACES

Perhaps the lesson for those who ask WWJD? is that *God is often in the most unpredictable places*. Is the picture becoming clearer? Jesus is always found in unexpected places: in the womb of a virgin teenager, in a manger, in a small and relatively isolated town like Nazareth, with unexpected people, while doing unexpected things.

Consider, for instance, the story that Mark tells about Jesus' encounter with a paralyzed man who by necessity relied on others for life's everyday necessities and now needed help with transportation. At the time, Jesus was visiting someone's home. Such a crowd gathered that there wasn't room for another person to enter the house. So when the group arrived with the paralyzed friend, they discovered that there was no way for them to get their friend inside.

I remember my mischievous impulses being aroused when first imagining this scene—simply stick your head in a window shouting "Fire!" and the problem is solved. Fortunately the paralytic was in the hands of more discerning companions, yet they were determined to get their friend in front of Jesus. They made their way onto the roof of the house and began ripping a hole over the spot where Jesus was standing.

I wish I could have seen the crowd's reaction. I suspect some were agitated by the disruption. "Hey, what's the deal? I got here hours ahead of time in order to get a good seat. Who do you people think you are? This isn't fair." Then, what about the owners of the house? Most of all I wonder what Jesus was thinking. I suspect he enjoyed the interruption.

If the determination of the demolition crew was not a rude enough shock, I'm confident that Jesus' unexpected response must have provided one. When Jesus saw *their* faith—that's plural; he's not talking about the paralytic but referencing the friends' role—he said to the paralytic, "Take heart, son; your sins are forgiven" (Matthew 9:2 NRSV). In other words, "It's time for you to be really free!"

Meanwhile, I suspect the group looking down through the hole was baffled. "What? Who said anything about sins? Not his sins, Jesus. It's his legs that are the problem."

Meanwhile at ground level another line of questioning must have begun to brew. In typical fashion, the religious specialists started arguing about Jesus' right to forgive sins with an arrogant, who-does-he-think-he-is? air, all the while disregarding the paralyzed man lying at Jesus' feet in the rubble.

Knowing what was cooking before lifting the lid, Jesus called a halt to the scribes' malicious misgivings with a revealing question: "Why do you think evil in your hearts? For which is easier, to say, 'Your sins are forgiven,' or to say, 'Stand up and walk'?" (Matthew 9:4-5 NRSV). Since words are generally easier than action, Jesus demonstrated his authoritative power. Leaving no room for confusion or doubt, Jesus uttered a few words and the paralyzed man stood to his feet, gathered up his bed and walked—or perhaps did cartwheels—home. Seeing that he could make the man walk, he obviously could forgive sin.

Jesus never encountered an illness he couldn't cure, a birth defect he couldn't overturn or a demon he couldn't get rid of. But he did meet religious critics and skeptics he could not convince or convert! Sadly, some of those who heard Jesus' clearest words and witnessed his most compelling actions tripped over their religious certainty and angrily stormed away. Some things never seem to change.

Meanwhile, Jesus healed the man, "so that you may know that the Son of Man has authority on earth to forgive sins" (Matthew 9:6 NRSV). Thus he demonstrated his ability to see beyond the surface of a person to the very heart of the matter. Jesus knew that spiritual heart disease has a far more devastating effect than physical, mental or emotional illness. This man who had spent his life horizontally on the side lines and was now enjoying a moment of vertical notoriety would still someday die. Jesus did not come primarily to heal sick cells but to heal sick souls.

UNFATHOMABLE WORDS AND ACTIONS

There are loads of stories that illustrate Jesus' unfathomable words and actions. The more I read them, the more convinced I become that his thoughts and ways are different from ours. On countless occasions his words and actions contradicted the expectations of religious folks, thus provoking enormous alarm and confusion. Consider these puzzling examples:

- After instructing his followers to cross to the other side of the lake, one of them said, "Lord, first let me go and bury my father." Instead of responding with predictably compassionate words, Jesus said, "Follow me, and let the dead bury their own dead" (Matthew 8:21-22 NRSV).

- Shortly after Jesus appointed the twelve apostles, he became so consumed with his work that there was no time to stop and eat. Demonstrating reasonable concern, his mother and brothers arrived to take charge, expressing fear that he'd lost his mind. When he was told his mother and brothers were waiting to see him, he callously asked, "Who are my mother and my brothers?" (Mark 3:33 NRSV). As if to emphasize his disregard for family ties, he added, "Whoever does the will of God is my brother and sister and mother" (v. 35).

- Surely someone claiming to be God would be expected to demonstrate respect for another person's property. However, when Jesus encountered a demon-possessed man and confronted the evil spirits that controlled him, Jesus gave them permission to enter a large herd of pigs, who immediately rushed down a steep bank into a lake and drowned. Thus, despite the value we would place on the rights of another person's property, Jesus encroached on somebody's property and livelihood (Mark 5:1-13).

- Rather than paying proper respect to the religious authorities, Jesus blasted them for being "whitewashed tombs, which on the outside look beautiful, but inside they are full of the bones of the dead and of all kinds of filth" (Matthew 23:27 NRSV).

- When people sought spiritual formulas and keys to success, Jesus gave them thought-provoking parables to ponder instead. Time after time, Jesus answered questions with more questions. Those who hoped for a pat on the back went away more perplexed than ever.

SCANDALOUSLY UNPREDICTABLE

These are just a sampling of the unpredictable ways that Jesus spoke and acted in the Gospels. They demonstrate that Jesus is not like us. He is a man of higher rights and powers. He is a divine mystery, the God-man, walking on our earth in our world of conflict. Thus, presuming we have God in our pocket and giving easy, glib answers regarding what Jesus would do in any situation is arrogant and dangerously misleading. To arrogantly presume that we're imitating Jesus is to act as if we are gods. As G. K. Chesterton said, "A great man knows he is not God, and the greater he is, the better he knows it."

I hope it's becoming apparent that it's not enough to merely ask, What would Jesus do? It may be enough if the goal is to be religious. However, Jesus' invitation to follow him and to live in union with him requires much more. We have to dig deeper and listen harder. We have to ask what Jesus meant by his strange words and actions. And what he meant is always more challenging than we can predict, more outrageous, more demanding. That's why his followers were so often perplexed, chasing after him and bickering among themselves as they tried to make sense of Jesus' latest puzzle.

I've concluded that the question Jesus would prefer is, What would Jesus have me do? (WWJHMD?) This is more in line with the Gospels. It's also more dangerous and demanding. I discovered a long time ago that there's a huge loophole in WWJD? Because Jesus is God, it's easy to offer that as an excuse when I attempt the impossible and fail. Jesus asks us to do the possible, that is, to be our true self.

When I think about my adult life, I'm grateful for the adventurous and meaningful work I've been given. For twenty-five years I endeavored to win the right to be heard by adolescents who had no interest in Jesus. The entire time I believed that no person has ever rejected Jesus, but rather a myriad of twisted misconceptions about Jesus. Since then, I've spent most of my time with followers of Jesus from a wide spectrum of faith traditions. Some are involved in local faith communities, large and small, and others have left the institutions they claim no longer, or never did, assist them in their faith journey

When I listen to these followers of Jesus speak of their relationship with him, they focus mainly on the rigorous challenge it is to be like him: loving unconditionally, offering forgiveness, providing hospitality, maintaining their personal spiritual habits, showing compassion for the poor and doing acts of kindness. Obviously, these are essential elements that we cannot ignore. However, these actions also provide us with some measure of recognition or gratification.

But I don't often hear what it costs to oppose religious traditions, to offend the religious community's standards, to challenge religious certainty or to hold Jesus' followers accountable to his values. Yet, these are part of being his follower too.

SPLITTING JESUS' PERSONALITY
What disappoints and troubles me most about my life is how often I deliberately split Jesus' personality, choosing the parts I wish to embrace and ignoring the rest. I need to be continually reminded not to pick and choose how I follow Jesus. There is a cost for following him, and at times the cost is sky high.

Jesus' candor regarding his aversion to religion is what led to his execution. The list of religious requirements he criticized is comprehensive. He opposed all formalism in worship, ritual purification, sacrifice, external prayer and fasting rules, sabbath and dietary codes, religious authority, the temple, and the harshness and rigidity of the Sadducees, Pharisees and scribes. The only thing he validated as authentic is the devotion of a heart in union with God, which he experienced and passed on to his followers. The Sermon on the Mount focused on these essential values.

And when you come before God, don't turn that into a theatrical production either. All these people making a regular show out of their prayers, hoping for stardom! Do you think God sits in a box seat?

Here's what I want you to do: Find a quiet, secluded place so you won't be tempted to role-play before God. Just be there as simply and honestly as you can manage. The focus will shift from you to God, and you will begin to sense his grace.

The world is full of so-called prayer warriors who are prayer-ignorant. They're full of formulas and programs and advice, peddling techniques for getting what you want from God. Don't fall for that nonsense. This is your Father you are dealing with, and he knows better than you what you need. With a God like this loving you, you can pray very simply. (Matthew 6:5-8)

This union with God that Jesus calls his followers to is not less demanding but more so. It calls for a radical cleansing of the heart that could never be achieved by externals alone. Therefore, he continually draws attention to the inner purity and union that mark a true follower's life:

You know the next commandment pretty well, too: "Don't go to bed with another's spouse." But don't think you've preserved your virtue simply by staying out of bed. Your *heart* can be corrupted by lust even quicker than your *body*. Those leering looks you think nobody notices—they also corrupt.

Let's not pretend this is easier than it really is. If you want to live a morally pure life, here's what you have to do: You have to blind your right eye the moment you catch it in a lustful leer. You have to choose to live one-eyed or else be dumped on a moral trash pile. And you have to chop off your right hand the moment you notice it raised threateningly. Better a bloody stump than your entire being discarded for good in the dump. (Matthew 5:27-30)

Jesus emphasized with his words and illustrated with his life that what is essential is not external but internal. He opposed religion because the religious took pride in their own efforts, were quick to judge and condemn, and were ready to impose burdens rather than share or lift them. Jesus opposed religion because the religious overlooked the poor and looked after the rich, despised the down-and-out, and prized the uppity. In a nutshell, those who followed religion thought they had God in their pockets.

A DAY WELL SPENT

About six months prior to the death of Henri Nouwen, I had the extraordinary privilege of spending a day with him and a small group of friends. Earlier that morning I had eaten breakfast with one of my colleagues who was encountering perhaps the darkest, most stormy weather of his life. When Henri arrived, our group was already seated in a circle. My friend was seated directly across from me; he and Henri had never before met.

After Henri was introduced, he entered the circle and offered a meditation about the synagogue ruler Jairus, who pleaded with Jesus to come to his home and heal his deathly ill daughter. Henri described how Jesus, moved with compassion, began making his way through the crowd.

Hidden in the throng of people was a desperate woman who had suffered from bleeding for twelve years. In addition to her pain, she had also exhausted all of her resources seeking a cure. Now under the cover of the crowd, she reached out and touched

Jesus' clothes. Immediately her bleeding stopped. Jesus stopped and asked who had touched him.

I suspect this was another one of those occasions when his followers were baffled by his unpredictable manner. "Why does he do these kinds of things?" they were probably asking each other. "Does he do this to embarrass us?" They reminded Jesus that countless people had touched him and therefore it was a pointless question.

Henri digressed to emphasize what he believed was one of the story's crucial points. "Jesus lived in uninterrupted and intimate accord with God. So much so that it's safe to say he was the most perceptive person who has ever lived. Therefore, he was alert to the hearts of people and keenly aware whenever God's power flowed through him to touch the life of another." Most peculiar were the words Henri repeated during the remainder of his meditation. "Countless times, I strongly suspect, Jesus knew what to do and say without knowing that he knew."

Henri described how the woman eventually flung herself before Jesus, identifying herself as the one who touched him. Then, reminding us of Jesus' mission to heal a dying girl, Henri emphasized how Jesus nevertheless chose to stop and listen to "the whole story" of the woman's twelve-year struggle.

It's not difficult to imagine how much time it must have taken, how many details the healed woman likely provided, and how helpless the waiting father must have felt. It's also not too difficult to imagine that something more than the woman's body was healed during those moments. What immense emotional, psychological and social suffering she must have endured; Jesus' healing of all of her being was an even greater gift. Over and over, Henri would repeat what was beginning to seem like a mantra: "Because of his uninterrupted and intimate accord with God, Jesus knew without knowing that he knew. He knew what he was called to say and do. He knew without even knowing that he knew."

Turning his attention away from the story and directing his compassionate eyes toward those seated in our circle, Henri insisted that the same can be true of us. "When we, like Jesus, live in uninterrupted and intimate union with God, we too become perceptive and know what we're called to say and do and even know without knowing that we know."

After driving the point home many times, Henri paused and invited the group to respond with questions or comments. After a long period of silence, he slowly turned and moved toward the friend I'd shared breakfast with. Although he was in deep pain, it was well-concealed. Stopping in front of him, Henri leaned over slightly and, smiling, asked, "How about you, my brother? Do you have any questions?" He shrugged and said nothing. Moving a bit closer, Henri smiled widely and said, "You have no questions?" I noticed tears begin to fill my friend's eyes; then speaking softly with a somber tone he replied, "I have a thousand questions." Instantly Henri knelt down, gently embraced him, grinned and jovially declared, "It's no wonder I felt drawn to you! So do I! So indeed do I! I have at least a thousand unanswered questions. Perhaps we need to become friends!"

I sat in stunned amazement. Henri had demonstrated the spiritual lesson he had been teaching us. Without knowing or knowing that he knew, he had tenderly approached a wounded soul and offered love.

PAUSE AND PONDER

- Do you tend to presume quickly what Jesus would have you do?
- Are you guided more by religious rules and habits than by God?

3   Beauty in Brokenness

"Nobody escapes being wounded. We all are wounded people, whether physically, emotionally, mentally, or spiritually. The main question is not 'How can we hide our wounds?' so we don't have to be embarrassed, but 'How can we put our woundedness in the service of others?' When our wounds cease to be a source of shame, and become a source of healing, we have become wounded healers."

HENRI NOUWEN

A while ago, I was invited to have dinner in the home of dear friends. Every week their extended family gathers for a simple meal. It was an extraordinary occasion for me to observe the quality of their lives together. Seated at the table were the maternal grandparents, two moms and dads, and five delightful, rambunctious children. At our feet sat three hungry dogs hoping for something to land at their paws. As the evening unfolded, words flowed (and sometimes flew); stories were told; memories were shared, some happy and others sad; ideas were expressed; and thoughtful questions were pondered. There was a generous, friendly, caring give-and-take that graced the entire evening.

The experience served as an ideal reminder that what happens during meals shapes a large part of our memories. As we grow older we naturally forget many things, but we typically remember the Thanksgiving or Christmas dinners with our families. We remember them with delight and gratitude, or with sorrow and resentment. They remind us of the love and peace that existed in our homes, or the hostility and conflict that never seemed to get resolved.

The dinner table has always been one of the most intimate and revealing places in family and community life. It serves as a barometer of our lives. If you really want to know what's on the heart and mind of a person, there's no better way to find out than to dine in his or her home. The dinner table has a way of dismissing pretense and promoting genuineness and sincerity, or exposing the fact that it doesn't exist.

Months later, I received a note from one of the people I'd shared the evening with. Reflecting back, she offered this candid disclosure: "As a young woman I thought everyone had it all together (except me). Now, at forty-two, I know we are all broken people living together in a broken world."

She was right when she acknowledged that we're all broken. The catalysts or causes for our brokenness don't have to be huge, tragic or devastating, though sometimes they turn out to be. Brokenness comes in all sizes and shapes, at the most inopportune times. When it comes, we often bury the pain and sadness somewhere deep inside, where it simmers and stews and gnaws at our peace, faith and joy. In the process we become even more broken.

Despite our attempts to keep it concealed, evidence of our brokenness seeps through and leaves its mark on all of life. The most notable dramatic productions and musical compositions, the most celebrated sculptures and paintings, and the most consumed books are often expressions of profound human brokenness. While knowledge of our brokenness is never far beneath the surface of our life, we experience most of our moments in deliberate denial of its presence and the reality of its life-altering effect.

MEMORIES BURIED DEEP WITHIN

Years ago at a workshop he was leading I heard author Gordon MacDonald explain how in late spring each year he would return to his New England farm to mow the lawn and ruin a mower blade on a rock that wasn't there the previous year. He explained that of course the rock had been there the previous year, beneath the surface, where it could do no harm. However, the deep winter freeze had a way of forcing some rocks to the ground's surface.

Like rocks forced to the surface by harsh and difficult conditions, memories of the most painful and dark experiences in my life, by God's severe mercy and grace, have surfaced in recent years.

One incident occurred when I was a young boy. I witnessed something that was undeniably vile, despicable and inappropriate for any child to see. Those who inflicted the wound were themselves wounded and meant no harm to me. Nonetheless the experience left me fearing that I was perhaps invisible to the people involved—people who were trusted guardians. As a child the only other option was unspeakably worse: I had no value or significance. Otherwise, why would they let me become a victim of their indiscretion? That was the most *de*formative and wounding incident to occur during my early childhood.

Driven by fear provoked by that trauma, I searched desperately for recognition and for ways to be loved and respected. Consequently I'll always remember the magical afternoon when the most drop-dead gorgeous girl I had ever seen looked into my eyes and smiled. We were in the seventh grade, and to my nervous delight our desks were side-by-side. Although I had studied her carefully and memorized every detail of what made her remarkable, I was certain that I didn't exist in her world.

She had long, blond hair, strikingly beautiful blue eyes and a smile worth dying for. Bored by the lesson, I was occupied with removing lint from my navy blue sweater when I sensed someone staring at me. I glanced in her direction and to this day I have remained startled by what I witnessed. This middle-school goddess was acknowledging my existence with the most redemptive smile that I recall ever seeing. Anxiously, I watched as she took from her notebook a piece of paper and began writing. As our teacher faced the front of the room the soon-to-be restorer of my soul reached across the aisle and handed me the note.

In that eternal moment, the words she wrote were seared onto my memory.

Dear Fil,

You are the neatest guy I've ever known. I like that about you. In fact, I like it a lot!

Love,
Lori

I recall at that moment thinking, *Holy smoke! She knows my name. She even knows how to spell it!* My heart was pounding and I panicked at the thought of her noticing my blushing face. I swear, had I died at that moment, I would have died a happy young man! *God I can't believe it! She says I'm the neatest guy she's ever known.*

Obviously, I didn't die. Instead, I began searching for ways to maintain Lori's apparent interest. I also decided that for the rest of my life, at least as long as Lori might be watching, I would be the "neatest" guy around. (I continue to find it difficult to wear my shirt-tail out and I'm constantly on the lookout for lint.)

Eventually, Lori and I headed in different directions. However, by that time my course in life had been set. Since then, I've spent a good portion of my life striving to know what "neat" looks like and what "neat" means to everyone that I've wanted to love and respect me. Living this way, I've been broken more than a thousand times by my repeated failures to measure up.

ANOTHER BETRAYAL

Years later my life was once again badly broken by another life-defining event. I was a high school senior and had been invited to attend a spiritual life conference with my pastor. Arriving late at a mid-morning session the only available seat in the crowded auditorium was in the front row. Discreetly I slid down into the empty seat next to an older distinguished gentleman as the speaker was being introduced. As the crowd began applauding the gentleman seated next to me rose and made his way to the platform.

He was an admired evangelical leader and powerful orator; I was mesmerized by the man and his message. After the session ended, as I was gathering my belongings and preparing to depart, the gentleman I'd just heard speak signaled for me to wait. He greeted me with a handshake and asked if I had plans for lunch. "You've heard what I have to say. It'd be a pleasure to hear your story."

I was astonished that someone so revered would be interested in knowing me. I was dazzled by his probing questions about my life and stunned when he expressed interest in my future as "a rising star with unlimited potential for service in God's kingdom." (You never forget remarks when you're starved, as I was, for recognition and approval.)

Over the course of the next couple of years we communicated on numerous occasions. His interest was enthusiastic and appeared sincere. His praise and affirmation of my giftedness was like rain falling upon a wilted flower.

During my junior year of college he invited me to accompany him on a preaching mission and to share the speaking responsibilities. I was flabbergasted by the invitation and his confidence in me. However, upon our arrival I was surprised to discover that we were sharing a room. Yet I was too insecure to express my uneasiness.

After returning to our room on the final evening of the conference, our conversation took a drastically abrupt and sharp turn.

Suddenly moving toward me, he began explaining that he could no longer resist acting on the raging physical attraction he'd felt since our first encounter. Although I was able to halt his inappropriate advances, it was an indescribably disturbing experience. The disappointment and disillusionment that followed were shattering.

This dreadful experience remains in my memory as a spiritual, emotional and psychological betrayal of epic proportions. Several months later while I was recovering in a hospital's psychiatric unit from the physical and emotional meltdown that today I believe was related to this trauma, he called to assure me that "if you ever make the foolish mistake of misrepresenting my wholesome interest in your future as a minister, I will personally destroy you." I never spoke with him again.

Nonetheless, I remained traumatized by the nightmarish encounter and wondered whether I'd ever be able to trust a person again. Thus my life became like a container of toxic disillusionment, shame, fear and brokenness. Unable to sort through the wreckage and to discern what to do with these deadly elements, I tightly sealed the bottle and buried it deep within my subconscious. I hoped that my memory of these horrid events would fade and that others would not detect that anything was wrong with my life.

A WORLD WITHOUT BROKENNESS

Like most of the people that I know, there are moments when I find myself yearning to live in a world without brokenness. While reading a local newspaper a few years ago I was captivated by the headline "God Knows, Suffering Is Part of Game." The journalist, Leonard Pitts, a favorite of mine who writes a syndicated column for the *Miami Herald*, began the article tongue-in-cheek. He began by explaining that he had recently hung out with God at the park, where they had played their regular game of one-on-one.

At the conclusion of their game, Pitts asked God to comment on a recent news event. Specifically, Pitts wanted to know if God caused an earthquake in India. Since God hadn't seen the paper, Pitts explained the situation.

> It seems this fellow named T. John, an official in the Indian province of Karnataka, was forced to resign over remarks he made in a speech to some students. He told them that a recent earthquake was an act of revenge by God for attacks by Hindus on the country's Christian minority. The quake claimed upward of 12,000 lives.

When God offered no immediate reply, Pitts asked God again if it was true. After another delay, God finally spoke, and Pitts offered this account.

> "Does T. John know anything about these 12,000 people?" He asked finally. "Do YOU? Can you tell me which ones persecuted Christians and which ones were Christians themselves? Or Moslems or Jews? Can you describe the ones who stole from the poor or mistreated children? Can you name the ones who gave bread to the hungry or read to the blind?"

Wisely, Pitts shrugged and acknowledged that he couldn't.

> God said, "I can. Those people didn't die for revenge."
> "Then why . . ." I caught myself, remembering how teed off he got with Job for pestering him with questions.

Admitting his relief, Pitts reports that then God smiled.

> The sun glanced through the clouds. "I know," he said. "You want a world without pain. A world without suffering and loss. But that would also be a world without healing, without joy and redemption. Each one gives meaning to the other."

Truthfully, I'm not sure Pitts has it right when he seems to say we have suffering so we can have redemption. I don't believe God created suffering. Humanity did. Nonetheless I appreciate his candor, playfulness and wondering about things that also make me wonder. And like Pitts there are times when I believe that God has spoken to me, and it's often been in the least likely ways and places. It seems that life's most dreaded and difficult challenges usher in the most longed-for and delightful opportunities.

This was the case a few years ago while I was sitting in a therapist's office with my wife and our son Will. I recall the counselor explaining that though our son's "presenting issues" were the reason we were meeting, in all likelihood unresolved issues would eventually surface in other family members' lives.

My lifelong struggle with outbursts of raging anger was much more severe than his age-appropriate adolescent struggles. For years, shame brought on by secrets, lies, betrayals, relationship breakdowns, disappointments, and unresolved yearnings for love and respect lay beneath the veneer of my life. The cancerous repercussions of denying, minimizing and spiritualizing my brokenness were immense. Caught in this trap, I was becoming progressively less the person God created me to be and more a poser.

Guess Who's Coming to Dinner?

The Gospel writers provide enlightening eyewitness accounts of eight instances when Jesus accepted an invitation to dinner. Three of these (the wedding at Cana, in the home of Martha and Mary, and the meal in Emmaus after his resurrection) were common social occasions shared among friends. The other five, however, broke every rule of social propriety and religious decorum.

Mark 14:3-9 relates one of those alarming occurrences when Jesus attended a dinner in the home of Simon the Leper. The epic drama began when a bottle of expensive perfume was broken and poured on Jesus' head.

Stringent laws enforced a harsh stigma against leprosy. Those afflicted with the dreadful disease (the modern equivalent of AIDS) were required to live outside the city walls and warn others that they were unclean. However, Jesus disregarded these rules and chose to have dinner in Simon's house.

> While he was in Bethany, reclining at the table in the home of a man known as Simon the Leper, a woman came with an alabaster jar of very expensive perfume, made of pure nard. She broke the jar and poured the perfume on his head. (v. 3 NIV)

I distinctly recall how the word *broke* first caught my eye, taking me into its grasp. When we're attentive to the primal pain that brokenness inflicts instead of living in denial, we tend to pay closer attention to the word whenever it appears. "She *broke* the jar." *Broke*. Such a plain and simple word that often describes cataclysmic, life-altering events. Whenever the word *broke* is spoken or written, it signals that something drastic has occurred.

The alabaster jar was neither the first nor the only thing that was broken. The woman had already broken the social rules and customs of her day. And Jesus soon joined her in the violation by coming to her defense.

Women had no place in public life. They were not to be seen or heard. Yet audaciously, compulsively and unwaveringly this woman broke social norms. Demonstrating a wildly passionate indifference to what the invited guests might think, she broke in upon the conversation occurring around the table.

Her outrageous and disruptive actions became the focus of everyone's attention. The consensus among the men was that her action was scandalously inappropriate and wasteful. Perhaps they imagined their outburst would win Jesus' favor. Exuding an air of confidence, they rebuked her harshly.

How Do We Do It?

Ever wonder at our certainty about what is in the heart of another person? Ever notice how often, according to Jesus, our conclusions are dead wrong? Have you detected how repulsed we religious people are by brokenness? Having been there, I know what I'm describing. To religiously oriented minds *brokenness* and *waste* are synonymous. We religious people always have a distinct preference for orderliness, decorum and predictably prudent behavior. We never overlook an opportunity to condemn those whose lives are messy, broken and seemingly out of control.

Not so with Jesus. Jesus is at ease with broken people. But those who are broken and don't know it or refuse to admit it provoke Jesus, especially when they begin attacking others. To the sanctimonious who were prone to aggression and harassment of others, Jesus made clear his values.

> Do not judge, and you will not be judged; do not condemn, and you will not be condemned. Forgive, and you will be forgiven; give, and it will be given to you. A good measure, pressed down, shaken together, running over, will be put into your lap; for the measure you give will be the measure you get back. (Luke 6:37-38 NRSV)

Informing those listening that they are as blind as those they are determined to reform, Jesus suggests they work on themselves before trying to fix anyone else.

Jesus willfully and deliberately embraced people that religion tells us to avoid. Jesus never distanced himself from people's pain. He openly connected with those who were being destroyed by their mistakes and foolish choices. Jesus dried the tears of the prostitutes, held the hands of the beggars, and touched the wounds of the sick and the deranged. He hung out with the defective people of the world and showed them what intimate union with God is all about. He was never interested in a person's title, society's label or the sign outside their place of work. Rich or poor, porn stars or preachers, gay or straight, Republican or Democrat—his Father, Jesus assured them, didn't give a rip. Instead, Jesus insisted, we're all God's children and in need of this shocking and amazing thing called grace.

Noting Jesus' openness and receptivity to those the religious elite cast aside, author Barbara Brown Taylor offers a practical explanation. "Their hearts are already broken, so it is not hard for him to get inside. But the *righteous are like vaults. They are so full of their precious values and so defended against those who do not share them that even the dynamite of the gospel has little effect on them.*" "I've had it with you! You're hopeless, you Pharisees! Frauds!" Jesus wails at them, "You keep meticulous account books, tithing on every nickel and dime you get, but manage to find loopholes for getting around basic matters of justice and God's love" (Luke 11:42).

"He cannot seem to make his point often enough" adds Taylor.

Self-righteousness kills not only those who are bludgeoned by it but those who wield it as well. Sometimes it kills them softly with gossip and cruel humor. Sometimes it works systemically, consigning some people to live in grim buildings with broken plumbing while others stroll neighborhoods of thick green lawns. And sometimes it works violently, getting people in the middle of the night to light torches and break windows.

Jesus does not preach humility because modesty is becoming. He preaches it because it is the only cure for the deadly pride and arrogance that make us want to kill each other, whether the murder is as subtle as purging someone from our circle of friends or as bloody as nailing someone to a tree.

The only cure for our brokenness is to stop playing charades, acknowledge our own and each others' brokenness, and become united by the only One who was broken in order to make us whole.

Herein lies the main reasons why the story of the broken jar has become so vital to me. It offers a clear picture of how my brokenness has opened the way for God to restore me to wholeness. It exposes the deadly flaw of relying on prescribed moral programs and religious requirements to mend my relationship with God. It brings me face to face with the profound truth that I don't have control over my life. I may fuss and fight and worry and rage and weep and barter and beg, but despite all my attempts, I'm incapable of living a perfect life. My life is undeniably broken, and only God can restore me.

Dreaming the Impossible Dream

I spent a miserable day in a cottage on the Oregon coast attempting to write a flawless introduction to this chapter. Finally, after countless failed attempts, I gave up. Exasperated, I paced the shore of an ocean as turbulent as my life, determined to find a perfectly whole sand dollar. I discovered hundreds that were broken, flawed or blemished, but failed to find one that was perfectly whole.

This is the story of my life: dreaming the impossible dream, striving to write the perfect introduction, searching to find the flawless seashell, yearning to be a neatly packaged person. My dream is to possess everything I want, to enjoy everything I desire, for all my wishes to be satisfied and my will to never again be frustrated or opposed.

It was my selfish longing for a perfect life (and escaping hell) that initially attracted me to the idea of a relationship with Jesus. Duped by the notion that Jesus promised me a life without brokenness, I set out on my faith journey buoyed by the belief that my troubles were going to cease. Finally, I was going to be given the life my heart had always longed for. After all, I had Jesus' assurance: "I came that they may have life, and have it abundantly" (John 10:10 NRSV). And the apostle Paul guaranteed, "So if anyone is in Christ, there is a new creation: everything old has passed away; see, everything has become new!" (2 Corinthians 5:17 NRSV).

However, despite the curb appeal of my interpretation of the gospel, I soon discovered that it is not even close to what God promised or intends for us. I've discovered the implausible promise that God has broken into our brokenness to find *us*, yet there is no guarantee that God will paste our messy, fractured life back together the way we want him to. To the contrary, brokenness is the key that unlocks the life we long for.

CRACKS THAT LET LIGHT SHINE

In her witty and irreverent portrayal of her reluctant journey into faith, Anne Lamott quotes a Leonard Cohen song: "Forget your perfect offering. There is a crack in everything. That's how the light gets in." I love the illumination those lyrics offer. However, I've appreciated it in an even deeper way since I saw the truth from another point of view. Cracks aren't only how the light gets into our dark and messy lives. They're also how light shines out of us to other people. And whenever I attempt to cover the cracks of my life, I cover up the light that shines through them.

Jesus' teachings convey that the life we've always wanted often is hidden in the midst of brokenness, that the simple life he offers often finds its beginnings in complexity. "Blessed are the poor in spirit" (Matthew 5:3 NRSV), Jesus said. "Heart-shattered lives ready for love," David wrote, "don't for a moment escape God's notice" (Psalm 51:17). On another occasion David declared what he had experienced firsthand: "The LORD is near to the brokenhearted, / and saves the crushed in spirit" (Psalm 34:18 NRSV).

The most authentic and meaningful friendship with God comes

through life's most shattering experiences. If grapes and grain are not crushed, there can be no wine and bread. If the seed doesn't fall to the ground and die, there can be no harvest. If our life is not broken, there will not be the deepest and best camaraderie with God.

This truth was illustrated a while ago when our family attended the funeral of one of my wife's aunts. During the eulogy it was noted that the early years of her life were marked by adversity and hardships. Yet, having endured them, she often declared, "There are just some things in life that, if they don't kill you, will help to strengthen you."

I believe she was right! Indeed, her tenacious, determined and persevering faith in Jesus Christ was honed, developed and deepened during those dark and difficult days. And so it is with us.

The life we really want and the future God wants for us are in all likelihood hidden in our biggest predicament, our worst failure, our deepest fear or our most dreadful disappointment. Despite how odd or outrageous it may seem, it's no less true: Brokenness, more than any other force in the world, has the power to mold our character into the unique shape God intended it to possess. Accepting the reality of my broken life is the necessary beginning point in becoming the person God created me to become.

LET'S FACE THE TRUTH: WE'RE ALL BROKEN

The truth that I am broken is the single most painful and difficult admission I've ever made. It's also the most truthful, honest and hopeful thing I've ever said about myself. Nonetheless, I've lived most of my life immersed in unreality, numbing the pain of brokenness through denial, blaming, rationalization, addiction and avoidance.

Meanwhile, where in the world did we ever get the idea that we're supposed to have our act together? How could we ever imagine that our lives are not broken? All we need to do is to take a look at the

Bible to see that its pages are overflowing with stories of brokenness. All of the biblical characters were broken. Each of them was a bizarre bundle of paradoxes, a complex mix of strengths and weaknesses. David, Abraham, Lot, Saul, Solomon, Rahab and Sarah were God-loving, courageous, brilliant, fearless, loyal, passionate, committed holy women and men who were also murderers, adulterers and manic-depressives. They were men and women who could be gentle, holy defenders of the faith one minute and insecure, mentally unstable, unbelieving, shrewd, lying, grudge-holding tyrants the next.

We might expect the characters of the New Testament to be an improvement, but they're not. This is especially true of the ones Jesus affectionately called his *friends*. Prostitutes, ragamuffins, head cases, tax collectors, adulterers, losers of all kinds—his disciples were hardly saints. They were impulsive, lazy, dishonest, disrespectful, selfish and so forth. The biblical characters of both Testaments were *broken*.

We're in good company! The Bible doesn't tell us to stop complaining and get our act together. Instead, the Bible unmasks the illusion of unbrokenness and calls followers of Jesus to come out of hiding and to stop pretending and stop feeling guilty, embarrassed and ashamed. The Bible makes us face the fact that each of us is deeply flawed and broken, and assures us that there are absolutely *no exceptions!*

PRESSURE TO PROJECT

The pressure to project an image of ourselves as stable and neatly packaged saints hangs over most of us like a dark, menacing cloud. It's only natural for us to feel guilty and ashamed for not measuring up. "Should haves" and "ought tos" litter the terrain of our lives. Meanwhile, the sad effect of denying, minimizing and ignoring our brokenness is that we have become less and less human, empty shells with smiley faces.

People who appear to have their life neatly put together don't make it any easier. You may have seen the bumper sticker that begins with the words "My life before Jesus" next to a pitifully sad face. It's followed by "My life after Jesus!" next to a wildly happy face with rainbows and flowers in the background. It's simply not true. Faith in Jesus Christ does not turn all your frowns upside down. Furthermore, it cruelly compounds the already painful struggles with shame and sadness many people suffer.

I speak from a deeply personal and painful experience. For years, shame, deception, lies, betrayals, relationship breakdowns, disappointments, and unresolved longings for unconditional love and respect lay beneath the veneer of my life. Sadly, the result of denying and spiritualizing my brokenness caused me to become less human and humane. Misapplied biblical truths damaged my closest relationships and kept God from transforming me.

Today my life offers proof that brokenness can be an instrument for positive change. Embracing my brokenness has allowed God's power to flow and thus transform my life. My faith in God's redemptive power has been restored. But when brokenness was ignored and denied, it had the power to destroy me. It can lead to addictions and madness and destruction. Nonetheless, without it we never grow.

This theme is played out repeatedly in the Bible. The ancient story of Joseph, whose brothers sold him into slavery, is especially illustrative. Years later, after discovering that Joseph was free and in a position of power, the brothers selfishly wondered, "What if Joseph still bears a grudge against us and pays us back in full for all the wrong that we did to him?" (Genesis 50:15 NRSV). Joseph assured them they had nothing to worry about and provided an explanation for his generous nature: "Am I in the place of God? Even though you intended to do harm to me, God intended it for good" (Genesis 50:19-20 NRSV).

DESPERATE FOR RECOGNITION AND APPROVAL

Several years ago I participated in a program to learn how to be prayerfully attentive and responsive to God's presence and guidance. I wanted to open myself more fully to God's presence in my daily life. At the same time I desperately wanted to be recognized by my peers as a person who was well ahead of others, having already arrived at my destination.

Throughout the program I diligently projected myself in the best possible light. Near the end of the two years, I had coffee with a person whose depth, kindness and gentle spirit I'd grown to admire. Most outstanding was her humility and openness about her struggles. Numerous times I'd heard her declare, "I'm a broken person who's grateful for the profound gift of Jesus' friendship."

Since she was a talented potter, I was delighted to hear of a gift she'd made for me. Opening the package I discovered that her creation was nothing like I'd expected. Enthusiastically she explained. "It's a beggar's bowl. Isn't it lovely?"

I don't recall the words that came to my mind, however I'm certain the word *lovely* wasn't among them. To me, it looked like a shabby, far-from-complete work in progress. Yet in her eyes, these were the characteristics that made it "lovely."

Accompanying the bowl was a card with these words from Psalm 31:12: *I have become like a broken vessel.* As our visit concluded, the words she offered remain as vivid in my memory as my view of the now-cherished bowl sitting on the table in front of me: "Fil, for God's sake, please stop hiding, avoiding, denying and despising your brokenness. Dare and believe that there is wonderful, redemptive beauty in it. Even the most broken things can become, once reconciled to them, a wellspring of insight and wisdom and strength for the journey that lies ahead."

READER'S DIGEST SELVES

Most of the time most of us are not our true selves. Instead, we're secrets to ourselves and mysteries to each other. We are *"Reader's Digest* selves." We have edited ourselves so often that we don't know the person we have become. In the process we have forgotten our true identity as beloved daughters and sons of God.

I have discovered the necessity of authenticity. I have found trusted friends who are willing to ask probing questions that invite my true self to come out of hiding: *Am I willing each day to come face-to-face with a self who wants to keep playing hide-and-seek, acknowledge my reluctance to admit who my hiding self is, and bring that shy, rebellious self into the light of Jesus, who patiently shows me who I was meant to be?*

Somehow I found the courage to risk being more authentic. In the process I discovered that the rewards for being my true self are often greater than the consequences of pretension. I believe the same is true for all followers of Jesus. The major battle confronting followers of Jesus is not issues like abortion, homosexuality and politics. The real front-burner issue is authenticity. When "outsiders" look at Jesus' followers, they long to see people living in intimate union with God who are unafraid of their blemishes, because their blemishes point to the unblemished character of Jesus, who loves us as we are, not as we should be.

My highest hope is for all of us to stop trying to fool others by appearing to have our act together. As people living in intimate union with God, we need to become better known for what and who we actually are. Perhaps a good place to begin would be telling the world—before the world does its own investigation—that we're not as bad as they think. We're worse. At least I know that I'm worse.

Let's get real. For every mean-spirited, judgmental thing some preacher has said, I've thought something nastier, more hateful and more cutting about one of my neighbors. For every alleged act of homophobia by my fellow Christians, I've done something stupid to demonstrate my manliness. For every brother or sister whose moral failure has been exposed, I've failed privately. No matter how boring followers of Jesus may appear to be to the outsiders, they don't know the half of it; trust me. I've spent countless weeks and months in hopeless boredom, surfing randomly through ads, blogs and *People* magazine because I wasn't willing or able to risk what God was calling me to. If we really believe the gospel we proclaim, we'll be honest about our own beauty and brokenness, and the beautiful broken One will make himself known to our neighbors through the chinks in our armor—and in theirs.

God uses our brokenness, reflected in our failures, heartaches, disappointments and betrayals, to reach out to the hurting people who surround us. What a freeing and comforting thing to discover: sharing our struggles, failings and brokenness can provide assistance to others!

REMODELING

Practically every Friday morning over the past twenty years I've met with a small group of men for the purpose of exposing the brokenness in our lives. One of those men, an orthopedic surgeon, recently described how the 206 bones in our body are constantly going through a process he called "remodeling." "However," he explained, "the process is intensified when a bone is broken. For that reason, after a break, we wear a cast because the bone is vulnerable to further injury. Eventually the bone ends up stronger than it was before the break." Most fascinating was his final observation. "Very rarely does a bone break in the same place twice, because it has become thicker and stronger at the point of the break than it was before."

Applying the principle to more consequential aspects of our

life, he added, "Almost like a broken bone that needs to be reset, God breaks us where we need to be broken. He breaks the arrogance and lust and deceit and anger and resentment in our lives, but he does it to 'remodel' us so that we're able to heal and become stronger and authentic."

For example, I have a friend who has recently suffered from depression. When he described the confusion, loneliness, darkness, shame and fear he's encountered, I listened and empathized. When I said, "Brother, I understand," he was able to trust that I really did since he's heard me speak of my own battle with depression. And when I told him that he might continue having to face the darkness but that he was never alone, he believed me.

I learned the applied principle from the people who have helped me confront the reality of my own brokenness in its various shapes and sizes. By God's grace, they've been open about their weariness and their anger as well as their victories and strengths. I pray that by God's grace I may become like them.

WAITING FOR GOD TO MEET US

The summer after our son Lee completed his sophomore year in high school, he spent a month in Ethiopia, which proved to be a transformative experience as he confronted the reality of brokenness and experienced some of its value. During this month he discovered the importance of waiting for God to meet us in our brokenness. Here are his reflections after his visit to Mother Teresa's Hospital for the Dying.

> I stepped out of the cab, breathed the damp diesel air and turned to face the gate. We entered through the bright blue façade and were greeted by a nun dressed in simple robes, whose shuffling sandals led us down a hallway toward the complex. Out of my pounding heart came the prayer "Break

me" whispered again and again, "I don't want to be the same when I leave this place."

We stepped into a large open room full of beds. I had never seen a room like this one before. One hundred faces waiting to see the Maker's. One hundred men awaiting their greatest fear and their greatest hope. The reality of death had a nervous grip on the air. I awkwardly approached one of the patients whose wide, frightened eyes told the story of his pain. I knelt down beside his trembling body to pray. How I wished for the faith of the apostles in that moment! The power to tell this man to stand up and walk out of that place, but my voice shook. I did not know what to pray for a man on his deathbed. I asked for God to have mercy on him, but must I really ask mercy of the God who is perfect grace? The depth of man's fall from the garden is measured not by his sin, but by his suffering. All the sins in that room may be forgiven, but the pain will remain as a bitter reminder of our separation.

There is nothing to do in a room like this one, but to wait for God. There is hope for eternity, and the debt of sins has been paid, but I long for the day when there will be no more suffering. No more AIDS. The day of Christ's return is coming, and if anyone truly understands the hurt of this world, let them pray it is tomorrow. Until that day, we all are waiting.

PAUSE AND PONDER

- How has your life been broken?

- What do you suppose would happen if you met your brokenness as you'd meet a beloved friend? What if instead of retreating from it, you lingered and asked your brokenness to help you grow?

4   What's a Picture Worth?

*"Our churches are filled with people who look contented and at peace but
inwardly are crying out for someone to love them . . . just as they
are . . . confused, frustrated, often frightened, guilty, and often unable
to communicate even within their own families. But the other people
in the church look so happy and contented that one seldom has the
courage to admit his own deep needs before such a self-sufficient group
as the average church meeting appears."*

KEITH MILLER

A while ago, a talented artist friend offered me the great
gift of his vulnerability through e-mail. He wasted no time getting
to the point. "Fil, I'm in the midst of a horrible crisis of faith."
Then he explained that his church had asked him to exhibit a self-
portrait for a special event. Rather than risk its meaning being
overlooked or misinterpreted, he also provided a brief written
explanation, which drew his pastor's ire. Apparently the pastor
felt that his disclosure was too honest.

The painting reflected his conviction that there's no room for
pretending in a Christian's life—acting like God is in control
when you don't believe that he is, giving the impression that
everything is all right in your life when it's not. His particular
concern was with religious people changing their appearance
when among other religious people in order to fit in or to be ac-

cepted as holy. *We are told that Jesus loves us as we are, sin and all, ugly bits and worthless bits. We are quoted clichés like, "Come as you are." We are offered relief from the burden of hiding in our guilt and shame. We are offered ultimate acceptance.*

The problem begins, from my friend's perspective, when we step through the doors of many churches. Suddenly we're confronted with an endless stream of things that are wrong in our lives, things to repent of, things that need changing. Meanwhile, the Bible instructs us, "Make this your common practice: Confess your sins to each other and pray for each other so that you can live together whole and healed" (James 5:16). Yet nobody does it, because that would mean taking off our mask of holiness. Therefore we live our lives jumping through imaginary hoops in order to be accepted by the very people who invited us to "come as you are."

He concluded his remarks with this bold pledge: "I refuse to wear a mask any longer! I will not pretend, not even for Christians. Wearing a mask will destroy you, even if it's a socially accepted Christian mask."

After reading the letter I opened the file containing his portrait. It was titled "A Broken Mask," and I was stunned by its force. Wearing an athletic jersey and baseball cap, he is seated and leaning forward with his elbow resting on his knee. His head is propped up on the backside of his hand. He appears downcast, gloomy and regretful. His eyes are transfixed and pensive as he gazes at a mask which he holds in his other hand. The mask clearly bears his likeness, yet its image tells a different story. The face is soft and serene, yet spirited and winsome. The bright eyes appear clear and hopeful. The mask portrays peace and freedom. Yet it's a lie.

For hours I remained at my desk feeling deeply distressed. Why does pretending become the craft of most Christians? When will we be freed from the dread of our fraudulent life being exposed? From the endless ways we painstakingly attempt to convince others of what we can't convince ourselves: that we are valuable? What will it take for us to stop living irrationally behind our frantic falseness that cunningly conceals who we really are? Are we so blind that we cannot see how our pretending drains every ounce of our integrity? Will we die before our denial, displacement and repression turns us into a shell of our true selves?

These haunting questions provoked an onslaught of images of members of Congress, priests, pastors and teachers, some of them friends who have fallen, crushed beneath the weight of their shameful secrets. Before I turned out the lights, locked the door and wearily headed for home I'd been reminded that a secret life of pretending never stays secret. I'd also wept for myself and all those who have suffered beneath the torturous, crushing weight of fear, guilt and shame that always accompanies pretending. As I plopped down into my seat and began the drive home, I kept wondering, *Can't there be another way?*

To Know Me Is *(Not)* to Love Me

Let's stop playing games. Can we finally be truthful, at least with ourselves? If so, let me ask you some questions that have confronted me—and my own masks.

Do you ever fear that if those who say they love you were given an opportunity to really know you, they would turn away and withhold their affection? Do you sometimes feel unlovable as the result of repetitive rejection? Have you foolishly or bravely chosen to risk being authentic and been met with the crushing realization that those who know you don't love you? How has this experience deformed your life? Have you then become a slick imposter, skillfully giving the impression that you are the mask you wear? Despite your "glittering image," do you live in confusion and fear behind the isolating walls you built for your protection? Have you deluded yourself for so long that pretending has become not only acceptable but necessary? If so, rest assured, you are not alone.

For as far back as I can remember, I've struggled with raging anger. Going back and forth between despising and denying it, and everything in between, I've done everything in my power to keep it in check. What I have despised most are the countless times my venomous rage has been grossly out of proportion with the provocation, and most especially when it was directed toward people who are most dear to me. A few years ago I swallowed enough of my pride and mustered up a sufficient amount of courage to visit a therapist for help.

One of the first things my counselor assured me was that anger is a good thing. "That's why," she explained, "it's all right that Jesus got angry in the temple." Next she helped me realize that just like red, yellow and blue are primary colors, and secondary colors can be made from a mixture of these, anger is not a primary emotion. Anger is a secondary emotion that is almost always a mixture of primary emotions. Our anger can be a message—a signal that something is going on beneath the surface. This is the G.I.F.T. of anger, indicating in all likelihood the presence of *guilt, inferiority, fear* or *trauma* in our lives. It offers the possibility of exploring and coming to know ourselves more fully. When we learn to use the gift of anger, we can step more fully into our true self. This is a gift to us and to everyone in our lives.

I returned home feeling relieved and hopeful. I also recall thinking, *if guilt, inferiority, fear or trauma are the triggers for anger, it's no wonder I'm so angry.* I was confident that all of these primary emotions were hidden within the dark recesses of my heart. After our next few sessions, I began to note how annoying her repeated questions regarding my childhood had become. *Why does she persist with questions about my past, when I've assured her there's nothing I'm intending to hide?*

Finally, one afternoon I had tolerated as much of her prying as

I could stand. Enraged, I angrily shouted, "I've told you that I have nothing I wish to hide! Why can't you believe me and give it a rest?" Immediately I felt stunned and embarrassed by my outburst. I also felt terribly lonely and afraid. Although I had wished to hide nothing, much had been hidden.

Her response was precise and direct. It reflected a genuine kindness and concern. "Fil, the gaps between your stories are huge, indicating that there are deeply buried, forgotten and untold segments. I believe the time has come for you to discover more of who you are, apart from the role you've been playing." It took me no time to realize that my outburst was fueled by my own fear of encountering what had been forgotten. Before our session ended she gently posed a simple question: "Do you have any pictures from your childhood? Perhaps looking at some old photographs and talking about the memories they invoke would help to resurface some forgotten memories."

Abruptly and unexpectedly the sound of my mom's voice began echoing inside my head. On countless visits to my parents' home, Mom had reminded me, "Son, before you return home, please make sure you have that shoebox I've been saving. It's filled with pictures from your childhood. For some reason you keep forgetting to take them with you."

Prior to my next session I called Mom and asked her to please mail to me the box of pictures. When I returned to see my therapist, I carried a single picture. It appears to be an innocent picture of a young boy, neatly dressed, standing next to his dad. Yet to me it's the most revealing picture that I've ever seen. An enlarged 8 x 10 copy sits framed on my desk. I carry a smaller laminated version wherever I go. It has become a window into my soul enabling me to see into my life as a child and understand how at an early age my soul was formed.

Taken when I was seven years old, it's a black and white print.

Decked out in our Sunday best, at attention with our hair combed neatly, we're a sight to behold. I'd dare to say that even with a search warrant, you'd be hard-pressed to identify anything wrong with either of us. We look, as some folks say, "picture perfect."

Our Sunday morning ritual actually began on Saturday night. After dinner, Mom would make certain that my suit was pressed and my shirt sufficiently starched. Meanwhile, Dad and I attended to shining shoes. Like a football team on the night before a big game, we religiously prepared the gear for our Sunday performance.

Once suited up on Sunday morn, Mom and Dad, my siblings and I piled into the car and headed for Winter Park Baptist Church. For reasons that my own three children helped me to understand, Mom or Dad always escorted me to the doorway of my Sunday school class. Before giving me a kiss and sending me inside, they'd repeat the mantra: "Now Fil, we've taught you how to behave. Don't you disappoint us! You know how to act!"

Recalling those days at the doorway and the Bible stories we were taught, the fact has occurred to me that the lesson was essentially always the same: "You've been taught how to behave. Don't disappoint us. You know how to act." Besides my parents, I never lacked teachers and preachers, neighbors and relatives reminding me *how to act*.

Is it any wonder that my understanding of what it means to be a follower of Jesus and live in relationship with God was as simple as following the rules, never disappointing anyone and acting appropriately? Although I'm confident that no malice was ever intended, as I grew older, my life sadly became *an act*.

WHAT'S A PICTURE REALLY WORTH?

The expression "A picture's worth a thousand words" is commonly accepted as true. Yet, though pictures may speak, they don't necessarily tell the truth! What we see is not always what we get.

At the turn of the nineteenth century the now familiar saying "A picture's worth a thousand words" was introduced by a marketing firm as a catchy sales promotion. The original saying, "A picture's *meaning* is worth ten thousand words," is an ancient Chinese proverb, yet its message was not precisely what was needed. So with a little tweak, it then conveyed the message they wished to deliver. Although the variation was slight, the change to its meaning was considerable.

A few years ago a major chemical corporation ran a series of advertisements designed to express their environmental concern. However, when the news media covered the story, they referred to a group of protesters who weren't convinced that the ad campaign reflected their true values. Among their signs was one that signaled their doubt and issued this challenge: "Clean up your act, not just your image."

The protesters' challenge echoes Jesus' bold confrontation with the Pharisees when he compared them to a dishwasher who cleans the outside of a container while leaving the inside dirty. To them he said:

> I know you Pharisees burnish the surface of your cups and plates so they sparkle in the sun, but I also know your insides are maggoty with greed and secret evil. Stupid Pharisees! Didn't the One who made the outside also make the inside? Turn both your pockets and your hearts inside out and give generously to the poor; then your lives will be clean, not just your dishes and your hands. (Luke 11:39-41)

Jesus was referring to the hand-washing ritual that Pharisees were devoted to before eating a meal. Of course, their concern was not hygiene but reputation. Yet Jesus is never fooled by appearances. He knew that the ritually neat, tidy and clean religion of the Pharisees didn't go beneath the surface. Their act was

good, but what went on behind the closed curtain of their lives
was bad.

AN INSATIABLE CRAVING

Tragically, religion trained me to be just like the Pharisees. By the
time I was in high school, my preoccupation with outward appearances took the form of an insatiable craving for acceptance. I
would do anything to gain the approval of the crowd. Actually,
crowds. I had two lives with two sets of friends, for whom I
adopted two very different standards of behavior. With my "godless" friends, I appeared godless, and with my "faith-full" friends,
I appeared faithful. It was a delicate balancing act, but I was adept
and learned quickly.

The strategy worked well. However, forty years later, I'm still
saddened by a shameful memory, one of the many diabolic moments that once defined my life. After getting drunk and attempting to take advantage of a young lady in a vulnerable, drunken
state, I stood with her at the door of her home. Before stepping
inside, she declared, "Fil, you certainly did correct my mistaken
image of you tonight. I always thought you were a follower of Jesus, but tonight you proved you're like most of the other religious
people I've known. Hell, you're just like the rest of us!"

As the fraudulent picture of me continued to develop, a picture
of God was also coming into focus. Like me, God possessed a public and private image. On the outside God was all love and smiles:
"This is how much God loved the world: He gave his Son, his one
and only Son. . . . God didn't go to all the trouble of sending his
Son merely to point an accusing finger, telling the world how bad
it was. He came to help, to put the world right again" (John
3:16-17).

I knew how easily people appear to be something they're actually not. I knew how diligently I'd kept my dark side hidden.

Though I'd fooled lots of people, God was not one of them. I hated myself intensely and was confident that God must hate me too. *How could God view my disgusting life and not be angry? Even revolted?* And I didn't blame God for having these feelings. The truth appeared plain and simple—*I despise me for being such a con. Why would God not also despise me?*

I Think I Can Fix This

Though it acquainted me with the concept of grace, religion trained me to overcome my weakness, get rid of my hang-ups, and achieve intimacy with God by sheer, dogged grit and determination. Thus I remained oblivious to the reality that my frantic striving to please God—jostling to win his favor and thrashing about trying to fix myself—was a colossal insult to God.

My approach to living was as outrageously absurd as that of the naive plumber who, after viewing Niagara Falls, declared: "I think I can fix this." My life became grossly deformed by my misguided image of a too-small god. Meanwhile, an equally erroneous perception of a too-big me made matters worse.

How I wish I'd taken to heart the wisdom expressed in Paul's letter to the Galatians:

> God isn't impressed with mere appearances. . . .
>
> We are not set right with God by rule-keeping but only through personal faith in Jesus Christ. . . . Convinced that no human being can please God by self-improvement, we believed in Jesus as the Messiah so that we might be set right before God by trusting in the Messiah, not by trying to be good. . . .
>
> I tried keeping rules and working my head off to please God, and it didn't work. So I quit being a "law man" so I could be God's man. Christ's life showed me how, and enabled me to do it. I identified myself completely with him.

Indeed, I have been crucified with Christ. My ego is no longer central. It is no longer important that I appear righteous
before you or have your good opinion, and I am no longer
driven to impress God. Christ lives in me. The life you see
me living is not "mine," but it is lived by faith in the Son of
God, who loved me and gave himself for me. I am not going
to go back on that. (Galatians 2:7, 15-16, 19-21)

Paul's early life gives positive proof that religion has only
enough power to change the appearance of things. Religion has
never been able to get down into and change anyone's heart. Saying prayers, reading Scripture, receiving Communion, being bap-
tized and performing acts of service may look good and may impress the people who observe what we do; however, God is never
fooled. It's both a humbling and freeing thing to acknowledge
there's nothing we can do that reaches beyond the appearance of
things. Only Jesus has the power and resources needed to change
what's inside us. Only Jesus has what's necessary to disintegrate
our fabricated life and help us live from our heart.

DISINTEGRATING OUR LIFE

For many of us, religion becomes a container that securely houses
"the rules" for successful living. The rules integrate our life, providing the answers to the how-to-please-and-appease-God questions that religion emphasizes. When this happens, our life is reduced to a set of principles, Bible verses, moral absolutes and
formulas, as if God is some kind of mathematical problem to be
solved. The unmistakable conclusion is that once the rules are
understood, we can relax and feel secure because God is no longer
a mystery or beyond our grasp. As long as we remain focused on
surface issues, life goes well. However, when we hit a stumbling
block or two, we face the emptiness of our interior life. Suddenly,

"the rules" no longer seem to apply, our life begins disintegrating, and we're forced to change.

Several summers ago, I was scheduled to join a group of men for our tenth consecutive annual retreat. Our host was Mike Yaconelli. Having adopted the moniker "Notorious Sinners," it seemed safe to assume these were men I could reveal my untidy life to. Nonetheless, I had strived to impress them with my piety and godly living. The night prior to my departure, there was a colossal crisis in our family that resulted in me profanely threatening to abandon ship. But when I called the group to explain my predicament, emphasizing that it "involved one of our children," I presented myself as heroic and self-sacrificing, dutiful even, for choosing to remain at home.

A few months later, when he and I were together, Mike demonstrated the skill of a surgeon as he laid me open, exposing the truth that I was certain had remained hidden. "Dude, when you chose to not attend the retreat, you may have missed the best opportunity you ever had to finally be given what you've always wanted! I know why you didn't come, and it wasn't that your family needed you. It was your enormous pride! You knew that if you remained at home, it'd appear that your family crisis was entirely about them and that they needed you to fix it. Man, you may have fooled them, but not me. Your life's a stinking mess!"

It was all I could do to keep my rage and terror in check. I was about to lash out when I noticed the tears in his eyes and the quivering of his lips as he rose from his seat and made his way toward me. Sitting down next to me, he asked with tender kindness, "Fil, what will it take for you to stop being controlled by the fear of being yourself? Won't you please come out of hiding, tell the truth and let yourself be known? When you let others see the real you, then and only then will you experience the love for which you've always yearned."

On numerous occasions I'd been awestruck as Mike passionately offered to large crowds the words he was now directing toward me. "Fil, accepting the reality of our broken, flawed lives is the starting point of living with Jesus, not because living with Jesus will mend our brokenness, but because we then stop seeking perfection. Instead, we seek Jesus, the one who is present in the brokenness of our lives."

Mike finally broke through my defenses, helping me understand that it's not until I admit my desperate neediness that I can see Jesus for who he really is, a loving, accepting, kind and forgiving Savior, Redeemer and Friend.

I knew then that Mike loved me in a way that few others ever had. He saw vividly my vulnerable and unlovable self, but he embraced me and assured me that Jesus, who has always seen me as I really am, loves me too. Before our visit ended, he recalled these words Jesus spoke: "If your first concern is to look after yourself, you'll never find yourself. But if you forget about yourself and look to me, you'll find both yourself and me" (Matthew 10:39). Then he said, "The essential question for you to answer each day for the remainder of your life is this: Am I willing to come face-to-face with the self that wishes to keep playing hide-and-seek? Am I willing to acknowledge my hiding self and bring that timid, unruly imposter out into the bright light of Jesus' love and mercy, who patiently reveals to me the self I was intended to become?"

Today I find myself captivated by the tenderness and care of Jesus as he continually unveils a way of living that arouses all the senses deadened by religious professionalism. At long last I'm discovering that there is a much more nurturing way to live, and I'm being beckoned into it.

FEARFULLY AND WONDERFULLY MADE
Several years ago our family received a memorable Christmas let-

ter. In the opening lines the sender spoke of a Christmas program featuring her two-year-old son and several of his classmates. Because her son has Down syndrome and his class consists of children with various mental handicaps, she admitted that she wasn't sure quite what to expect. "What sort of program could there be when most of these precious tots are non-verbal?" she wondered.

When the curtains opened and the music played, she said her son "clapped and 'sang' and hollered in delight as one of his classmates sat at the front of the stage banging on a drum." As the program progressed to the older students singing and reciting their lines, our friend portrayed her emotion-packed experience in these words:

> I let my tears fall freely. My first thoughts were of sadness for all the imperfections that were on that stage, for all the "could have beens" had it not been for their handicaps. I wondered for a moment about the purpose for this annual Christmas program. Then a handsome young man with Down Syndrome, dressed in a tuxedo and top hat, came forward and sang "Surely the Presence of the Lord Is in This Place." Although some of his notes were flat, God spoke to me there.

At this point in the Christmas letter God spoke to me: "Fil, although you pity people like these, you'd be much happier if you became like them . . . simple-minded, open-hearted and uninhibited . . . if you'd simply lose your preoccupation with what others think about your appearance and performance."

Our friend concluded her letter with this simple reminder,

> God says that we are all created in God's image, "fearfully and wonderfully made." In Christ, we are perfect in God's sight. These people before me, filled with their afflictions, were doing exactly what God had created them to do—to

enjoy life, to love one another and to be grateful to their Creator. They were doing just that! Oh, if only we could be more like them.

If only . . .

Have you forgotten how to live from your heart? Tragically, most of us shut down our hearts in childhood. Instead, we learn how to manage our hearts to sufficiently function in society—and even to succeed! With desperate and determined striving, we make our mark on society. We cultivate a career, perhaps we establish a marriage and family, and we accumulate nice things and obey the rules while pretending that all is well with our heart. But our life of pretending isn't enough for our heart to live on.

What would occur in your life if you allowed your longings to open up in a more pure and transparent way so they could be healed and redirected? What difference would it make if there were a radical and ongoing shift within your soul's operational system—a shift away from the frantic striving to *achieve* intimacy with God toward simply opening yourself to receive God's gift of intimacy?

The changes would be considerable if your attention shifted away from what you feel you *must do* to what God has *already accomplished*. The enormous pressure to rely on your own too-limited resources would be relieved if you were able to draw on God's boundless supply. Consider the colossal burden of concentrating on the *ought tos*, *shoulds*, *have tos* and *musts*. It's time to leave that life behind.

Too many people are accustomed to feeling the crushing weight of bondage, duty and obligation while God wants to give them freedom. Life is not meant to be awkwardly lived from the *outside-in*. God designed us for living from the *inside-out*. We no longer need to feel pressure to *do* certain things in order to *be* in relationship with God. Religion produces horrendous feelings of shame and despair, but God's gift of grace is intended to produce a much different kind of fruit—rest.

An Unanticipated Lesson

I recall when my Boy Scout troop went to a week of summer camp. After settling into our quarters, we were instructed to report to the waterfront to have our swimming ability assessed. Well, I'd grown up on the coast and spent most of my summers in the water, so I had no concern. After swimming the required distance, I was instructed to float for three minutes. *What a joke*, I thought. *This'll be a cinch*—or so I thought!

The water I was accustomed to floating on was salty. But this was a freshwater lake, and I kept sinking! My sinking led to flailing, and when flailing didn't work, panic ensued. The lesson was simple: floating *works* only when we do nothing but trust the water to buoy us. However, if we don't trust the water to *hold* us, we naturally try to keep ourself afloat. My attempts to do it myself resulted in failure. In other words, floating is like a gift we can only be given; it's never achieved by striving.

We flounder and flail with many things: with our life in God, with what matters and why, with how to nurture our faith. We struggle with understanding how Christ's commitment to us changes our goals in life, and the way we then relate to others. All this high-stress flailing begins to subside with the gift he offers, and it continues to diminish as we're changed by the force of this undeserved gift.

In this new season of my life, I have very little interest in defending things that used to matter most. Zeal for my beliefs and improving my behavior, in particular, are at an all-time low. Like Barbara Taylor Brown, what now holds my attention is not "the believing parts but the beholding parts."

Beholding is more compelling and has captivated my attention.

Held within their spell, I seem to have a cataclysmic change unfolding inside me.

Behold the works of the LORD. (Psalm 46:8 NASB)

Behold, I will create
   new heavens and a new earth.
(Isaiah 65:17 NIV)

Behold, I bring you good news of great joy.
(Luke 2:10 NASB)

Behold, the Lamb of God. (John 1:29 NASB)

Behold, I stand at the door and knock.
(Revelation 3:20 NASB)

Behold, I am coming soon! (Revelation 22:7 NIV)

After years of serving a religious system incapable of delivering the kind of relationship with God I was designed for, I'm finally beholding Jesus. And God's unconditional love, kindness and care exceed all that I ever dared to hope for or imagine.

FULLY, BRAVELY AND BEAUTIFULLY

In his essay "The Killing of Time," Frederick Buechner offers this poignant observation: "We tend to live as though our lives would go on forever. . . . One life on this earth is all that we get . . . whether it's enough or not enough . . . therefore, the obvious conclusion would seem to be at the very least, we're fools if we don't live it as fully and bravely and beautifully as we can."

I've not found a more delightful description of the kind of life I sought with God. Aren't these qualities true of Jesus and his authentic followers? Isn't this a grand description of the life Jesus promised when he said, "The thief comes only to steal and kill and destroy. I came that they may have life, and have it abundantly" (John 10:10 NRSV)?

Fully. Thinking of living *fully* brings a variety of people to mind. They share several values in common, which, when woven together, produce a life of fullness. First, they're *grateful* for God's abundant care. Acknowledging all they've been given quenches the longing for more and opens the door to *simplicity.* Living simply and in gratitude doesn't diminish their life but makes it fuller, yielding both internal and external *order.* The well-ordered life, which is detached from the world's weapons of mass distraction, produces *peacefulness* and heightens their *alertness* to the presence of God. And their sense of God's presence generates profound *joy.* Now that's living *fully!*

But how does this happen?

In the prologue to the Gospel of John we read, "What came into existence was Life, / and the Life was Light to live by" (John 1:4). Jesus radiated life and lived it fully. He wasn't a boring preacher or withdrawn hermit; life flourished in his presence. When he spoke, something happened; something came alive in those listening. In Jesus the meaning of life becomes apparent. We live fully only when life is streaming into us, and that occurs only because Jesus came and continues coming.

Bravely. One of Scotland's greatest national heroes, Sir William Wallace, exemplifies bravery. One of my favorite scenes from the film *Braveheart* occurs when Wallace, played by Mel Gibson, addresses his faltering army before a great battle: "All men die, but few men really live." His words echo a life lived bravely.

By God's grace I too am being shown how to live bravely. It hasn't come easily but requires huge amounts of shame and pain and sadness due to pretense: pretending that I believed when I doubted, hiding my imperfections, maintaining the image of an ideal marriage with healthy and well-adjusted children when our family was dysfunctional. I finally got tired of the vast discrepancy between the appearance and the reality of my life. Thank

God I finally came to terms with how lost, soul weary and exhausted I had become. I had tragically succeeded at impersonating bravery, but on the inside I was cowardly, afraid and nearly dead.

Just a few years ago Jesus convinced me that the main barrier between us was my damnable good reputation. Most days my greatest concern was trying to impress others. I was constantly calling attention to myself, worrying how my actions would be interpreted or anguishing over whether my efforts were good enough. One of the most freeing moments of my life occurred when Jesus assured me that I'm lovable only because he loves me, and he always expects more failure from me than I expect from myself.

One of the biggest surprises has been that Jesus doesn't tell me what to do; instead he persists in telling me that he loves me. He's not interested in emphasizing rules and correcting my behavior, but invites me to walk closely by his side. Unlike an overprotective parent, he doesn't protect me from the dangers of living bravely. Instead he leads me to some wild places. Those who bravely follow him there experience the wonder-full life.

Beautifully. There's nothing more beautiful than the transparency of those followers of Jesus who refuse to pretend to be anything but who they are. That's the compelling and endearing quality that actor Tom Hanks brilliantly portrays as the title character in the movie *Forrest Gump*. Despite his limitations and deficiencies, Gump was his true self. He embodied the admonition "Be who you is, 'cause if you ain't who you is, you is who you ain't."

It's remarkable to encounter those whose life reflects the grace of a deep spiritual walk. They're neither arrogant nor proud; they accept their limitations with humility and transform difficulties into opportunities. Their motives are pure, their heart is kind, and they live above criticism.

We'd be wise to recognize the source of their beauty and subject ourselves to that source so that we too become not like them but

rather our own true self. Jesus declares that we're accepted unconditionally by God, and he guarantees that love drives out all fear.
Jesus lives out God's love for me so convincingly that I may cast
aside all fear associated with being my true self. Jesus is the visible
expression of the message that

> God is love. When we take up permanent residence in a life
> of love, we live in God and God lives in us. This way, love has
> the run of the house, becomes at home and mature in us, so
> that we're free of worry on Judgment Day—our standing in
> the world is identical with Christ's. There is no room in love
> for fear. Well-formed love banishes fear. Since fear is crip-
> pling, a fearful life—fear of death, fear of judgment—is one
> not yet fully formed in love. (1 John 4:17-18)

Jesus is the incarnate love of God. When love permeates us we
are whole, redeemed and free to be our beautiful true self. This is
the hope that inspires me. This is the foundation and the love on
which I live.

PAUSE AND PONDER

- Have you forgotten or perhaps never known how to live from
  your heart?

- What difference would it make if there was a radical shift within
  your soul from frantically striving to achieve intimacy with
  God to simply opening yourself to the unwarranted offering of
  God's gift of intimacy?

5   Right Rules or Right Relationship?

"Religion is the archrival of intimate spirituality. . . . Religion, a tiresome system of manmade dos and don'ts, woulds and shoulds— impotent to change human lives but tragically capable of devastating them—is what is left after a true love for God has drained away. Religion is the shell that is left after the real thing has disappeared."

DOUG BANISTER

The story of your life reminds me of the day I won the wrong race."

The curious comment came while I was seated with two friends on a brightly lit stage in front of a large audience. I had just described how it had taken me three decades of pursuing a religious life to realize that my pursuit was not taking me deeper into a nurturing and life-giving relationship with God. Instead, it had left me spiritually bankrupt and emotionally drained.

He shifted his weight and leaned forward with perceptive eyes; I sensed that this was going to be a doozy of a story.

"At the time, I was a scrawny high school sophomore. To my amazement I'd made my school's track team." (I didn't have the heart to interrupt him with the news, "Bob, anyone who tries out makes the track team.") Instead, I continued to listen with curiosity.

"I'd come to my first meet, with no idea whether I'd be given a chance to compete in an event. To be honest, I wasn't entirely certain that I wanted to. Then, without any advance warning, I heard the coach call out my name, 'Hey Bob, start getting ready for the next event. I want you to run the 400.'

"*Man,* I remember thinking, *Run the 400! What's the 400?*

"Following me onto the track where the other runners had begun assembling, my coach put his arm around my neck and with an air of confidence, said, 'Bob, this is the perfect event for a runner like you. Just once around the track. You can do it. I believe in you. Now get out there and win the race!'

"The next thing I knew, I was taking my place among the other runners. Each of them appeared to me, given my lingering prepubescent condition, to be fully grown men. Nervously occupying my place in the designated lane, I positioned my feet in the blocks. Suddenly the gun sounded, indicating the start of the race, and with an enormous surge of adrenalin propelling me, I started blazing my way down the track.

"My coach's confidence, the size of my competition and my inexperience left me certain the stage was set for my first high school humiliation. As we approached the first turn, I was shocked to discover myself in first place. Still lacking confidence, I anticipated that at any moment I'd be passed by the other runners. Yet, as I made my way down the straightaway, to my amazement, I held the lead. Imagining the unimaginable, I could already see the headlines in the following morning's news: 'Sophomore Sensation Wins 400, Setting New School Record.' Then suddenly, my brain received an urgent word of warning, dispatched by a terribly upset stomach: 'Dude! The pizza you ate at lunchtime is about to make another appearance!' The next thing I knew, my lunch had egressed, and I was sprawled out on the track."

Where in the world is he going with this story? I anxiously wondered.

"The next thing I remember was the stampeding of the other runners as they raced past me, some of them laughing, and headed for the finish line. Meanwhile, there I was, laying face-down on the track, wondering how, if there really was a God, this could ever have happened. My next thoughts were about whether my parents would support the plan I'd already begun fabricating: There can't be any doubt. I've got to transfer to another school before the morning bell rings tomorrow!"

Like most people, I have my own collection of *most humiliating* memories from high school; therefore my heart immediately went out to Bob. "So, how did you recover from this nightmare?" I asked.

"Obviously, this could have become what your question suggests. However, I've chosen instead to take the 'high road.' Rather than remembering the dreadfully humiliating day I failed to finish the 400, I've chosen instead to recall that truly triumphant day when I stunned the crowd by winning the 300! The only problem is: The race I won was not the race I was running, and what good is there in winning the wrong race?"

What a profound statement! *The race I won was not the race I was running.*

What an astute question! *What good is there in winning the wrong race?*

Bob hit the nail on the head! By telling his story, Bob illustrated the meaning of my life's story. Although I'd managed to win the race, the race I'd won was the wrong race.

Just like Bob, I have my own stories about crashing and burning, and being left with a horribly empty feeling. I've wondered what good there is in winning the wrong race. Isn't this precisely what Jesus was talking about when he asked, "What kind of deal is it to get everything you want but lose yourself?" (Matthew 16:26). That sounds to me a lot like winning a race and then discovering it was the wrong race.

BECOMING UNRULY

My religion, that meticulous system of right beliefs and behaviors that provided structure, support and guidance when I was growing up, and Jesus, who recklessly invites people to follow him into an intimate relationship with God, are not mutually exclusive. But they are clearly distinct. My religion comprised many good things. It taught me truths that I'm still convinced are important. It introduced me to values and principles that led me into plenty of worthy endeavors. Nonetheless, it also led me into an entirely wrong race.

The pathology of my religion erupted in insidious fashion: believing and doing the right things became a *substitute* for living in right relationship with God. As a result, I got lost in the details and simultaneously lost my heart. I spent most of my time learning what I *couldn't* do instead of celebrating and enjoying what I *could* do because of my relationship with Jesus.

Have you ever noticed how every time Jesus' followers began making rules (no children near Jesus, don't let the crowd get too close to Jesus, don't let people waste expensive perfume), Jesus intervened. "Back off!" I can hear him saying. "You still don't understand! How many times do I have to tell you what matters most? My message is plain and simple: Follow *me*."

Jesus' insistence that children have an advantage in following him is perplexing to followers of religion. They work long and hard to develop rigid and demanding codes of conduct. They place the cookies of a relationship with God on a shelf too high for children to reach. Therefore they get perturbed when Jesus foolishly moves the cookies so that children (anyone) can reach them.

> Jesus called over a child, whom he stood in the middle of the room, and said, "I'm telling you, once and for all, that unless you return to square one and start over like children, you're not even going to get a look at the kingdom, let alone get in.

Whoever becomes simple and elemental again, like this child, will rank high in God's kingdom." (Matthew 18:2-4)

A religious devotee has to wonder, *What is the big deal with Jesus and kids?*

One of the surest things about children is that they are born *unruly.* Yet the process of domestication and socialization begins immediately, especially in our churches. Children are taught how to behave, how to get in step with the cultural norms, how to act appropriately. Children are taught that understanding the rules and acting responsibly is what growing up is all about.

But I wonder if Jesus would agree?

I suspect Jesus would explain that in the process of teaching our children to follow the rules, we've diverted them from following *him.* Thus our emphasis on following the rules has trained them to live from their *heads,* where the rules are stored, rather than from their *hearts,* where their God-given and God-guided intuition resides. Somehow, we must enable our children to wisely discern when to follow the rules and when to break them, as Jesus himself did.

After the woman, like a child, broke her jar of perfume and anointed Jesus' head with the fragrant contents, some men indignantly asked, "Why this waste of perfume? It could have been sold for more than a year's wages and the money given to the poor" (Mark 14:4-5 NIV). And they rebuked her.

This irrationally extravagant woman broke the religious rules— first by barging into a dinner party uninvited and then by disrupting the evening with her wastefulness. Her actions were scandalous and inefficient. They had every reason to be incensed and to reprimand her severely. *What is this foolish woman thinking?* they must have wondered as they waited for Jesus to set her straight.

They were stunned when Jesus abruptly commanded them,

"Leave her alone" and then asked, "Why are you bothering her?" Their *minds* reeled when Jesus emphatically declared, "She has done a beautiful thing to me." It's abundantly clear that her extravagant affection sprang from deep within her heart and touched something deep within Jesus'. Although I sense that she offered her gift expecting nothing in return, it was undoubtedly exhilarating when Jesus pledged, "Wherever the gospel is preached throughout the world, what she has done will also be told, in memory of her" (Mark 14:9 NIV).

MANAGING MY GLITTERING IMAGE

Looking back on my life, I recognize that I cut out a whole lot of living by playing it safe and striving to follow the rules. And if that wasn't bad enough, I didn't succeed in the attempts, despite my earnest efforts. My failure became a source of shame and disappointment, which drove me to become scandalously deceptive. Terrified with the fear of being exposed, I diligently managed my glittering public image, which prevented me from trusting Jesus to accept me for who I was.

What a horrible tragedy! What a gross misunderstanding of who Jesus is and what he intends! After all, Jesus is the best teacher on when and how to *break* the rules! He touched lepers, healed on the sabbath, forgave people of their sins and hung out with people who failed miserably at following the rules.

I now clearly see how my striving to salute every rule that my religion ran up the flagpole caused me to enter the wrong race, which makes me angry. Yet for too many years it has been anger without an object, and I'm hoping this book will bring its end. I believe everyone involved in my religious instruction had the very best intentions and I'm certainly not aware of any intended malice.

The single thing that my religious training failed to impart is the vital truth that intimacy with God is more than religion. Union with God is more than behavior. Regardless of their god's name, all religions share this one fundamental distinctive: their followers are striving to climb a stairway to heaven, trying to reach and please God through their own efforts. But Jesus' teaching violently breaks rank with that worldview by embodying the reality that God is, inexplicably, reaching down to us! Although this is comforting to those who have tried and failed to get their life together, it's devastating to those who prefer religious striving.

The union Jesus invites us into is a profoundly relational encounter and not a religious treadmill. It begins when we say yes to Jesus' insightful questions, "Are you tired? Worn out? Burned out on religion?" and accept his gracious promises, "Come to me. Get away with me and you'll recover your life. I'll show you how to take a real rest. Walk with me and work with me—watch how I do it. Learn the unforced rhythms of grace. I won't lay anything heavy or ill-fitting on you. Keep company with me and you'll learn to live freely and lightly" (Matthew 11:28-30).

Sometimes I wonder, *What if I'd questioned the rigorous and inflexible demands of my religious system rather than questioning my failures? What if I'd challenged the source of the relentless pressures and demands instead of challenging myself to "get with the program and strive even harder to win the race"?* I wonder how different my life would have been if I had dared to poke around the edges of other people's apparent success rather than accepting appearances. Instead, I floundered in self-contempt, constantly belittling and condemning myself for being such a weak, miserable failure.

The distinction being portrayed is certainly nothing new. God has always been alert to the certain dangers of religion, and the religious fanatics of Jesus' day were astutely aware of the threat he presented. Jesus caused a commotion that threatened to undemine the delicate religious and political balance of power in Israel. While the authorities were precise and exacting, Jesus had a reputation for being unpredictable and doing the inexplicable. Yet he spoke with an air of authority as he shifted attention from external matters of religion to internal attitudes of the heart. Jesus taught that God isn't looking for people who are doing well in their religion, but for people who recognize their dependence on God.

What an inconceivable paradox that Jesus, this man the religious system sought to destroy, was at the same time gaining the affection of the "bedraggled, beat-up, burnt-out, sorely burdened, wobbly, weak-kneed, inconsistent, unsteady, poor, weak, sinful men and women with hereditary faults and limited talents, earthen vessels who shuffled along on feet of clay, bent, bruised, stupid, scalawags." These are the types of people whom Jesus proudly embraced and affectionately spoke of as his little brothers and sisters and friends.

When I compared the wholeness that Jesus produced in people's lives with the deforming effect of my religious system, the diametrical distinction became apparent. And as the truth came into focus, I concluded something was horribly wrong, and I was convinced that Jesus is *not* the problem!

WHAT'S THE DIFFERENCE?

The Pharisees were the most highly educated theologians and staunchly religious people of their day.* They were as familiar with the Scriptures as the backs of their hands. Yet sadly, many never allowed God's transformative words to penetrate their hard and misshapen hearts. Certain that they understood the will of God and had exclusive authority to act as God's agents, they were a menacing threat to those most vulnerable to the deficiencies of their religion.

Nothing about Jesus was more offensive to the Pharisees than his gracious receptivity of those whose lives were broken and

*See endnotes.

messy. Equally disturbing was Jesus' hostility toward the Pharisees' religiously neat and tidy lives. It was apparent that anyone who followed Jesus would not need religion. While the Pharisees were obsessed with obedience to God's law (and the subsidiary laws they added), Jesus scandalously taught that God would forgive even the most flagrant offender.

The Pharisees diligently adhered to a rigorous system of individual achievement. Personal responsibility left little room for personal response. Believing they could follow the demands of the Mosaic law, they convinced themselves that they were superior, worthy and blameless. Proudly, they imagined their exclusive right-standing with God as both hard-earned and well-deserved—a just reward for their vigorous adherence to the Scriptures and a large body of oral tradition that applied the law of God to the details of daily life.

Jesus didn't reject the Pharisees outright; indeed he actually had very good relations with individual Pharisees. Yet to the Pharisees' great chagrin, Jesus did nothing to validate their complex system or praise them for their tireless efforts. Appalled by their blind arrogance, Jesus launched a direct assault, an all-out frontal attack on the sightless Pharisees' trivialized notion of God. Jesus was horrified by their impression of God as a manageable deity certain to be impressed with their achievements. Outraged that they had diminished his Father, the Almighty, to a nitpicking scorekeeper, Jesus called their bluff, calling them "snakes," "hypocrites" and "blind leaders of the blind." In other words, they were winners of the wrong race.

Years later, a Pharisee who set out to destroy the movement Jesus set into motion abruptly became its champion. Physically blinded by the bright light of God's incomprehensible love and mercy while traveling to Damascus, Paul's impaired spiritual vision was radically transformed. He was now able to see the indisputable truth that Jesus Christ is superior to all religion. With equal passion, now redeemed and redirected, the apostle Paul declared that the strictest adherence to religious laws could never correct blindness or fill the emptiness of a human heart. In a number of letters Paul explained the limited power of the law, that it exposes the crookedness of our lives, our blindness to the truth and our need for a solution much greater than religion.

When we're so blind that we can't recognize God standing right in front of us, we can't see *anything* clearly. Everything is a blur! What tragically followed for the Pharisees was a drowsy indifference to matters of utmost importance and a fanatical obsession with trivial pursuits.

Despite their vast differences, the Pharisees' and Jesus' views were not mutually exclusive. Both emphasized the importance of believing the truth and how belief influences behavior. The Pharisees were "good people." They read the Scriptures. They did good deeds. And they *thought* they knew God. Yet they didn't love God; they loved the law and religion instead.

Nothing was more outrageous to the religious elite than Jesus' scandalous accusations toward them. Equally scandalous was street people's attraction to Jesus. Barefaced sinners were among his closest friends. Even Pilate, the pagan Roman governor, gave Jesus more consideration and benefit of the doubt. The rule keepers, however, were his most bitter enemies. Eventually the Pharisees became convinced that the world would be a better place without Jesus. Certain that they were doing God a favor, they began plotting a means to his end.

JESUS, WHAT ARE YOU HERE FOR?
Matthew's first encounter with Jesus illuminates the radically distinct difference between Jesus and the Pharisees.

> Passing along, Jesus saw a man at his work collecting taxes. His name was Matthew. Jesus said, "Come along with me." Matthew stood up and followed him.
>
> Later when Jesus was eating supper at Matthew's house with his close followers, a lot of disreputable characters came and joined them. When the Pharisees saw him keeping this kind of company, they had a fit, and lit into Jesus' followers. "What kind of example is this from your Teacher, acting cozy with crooks and riffraff?"
>
> Jesus, overhearing, shot back, "Who needs a doctor: the healthy or the sick? Go figure out what this Scripture means: 'I'm after mercy, not religion.' I'm here to invite outsiders, not coddle insiders." (Matthew 9:9-13)

Matthew could not have made the purpose for Jesus' coming any clearer: Jesus came for sinners—for the tax collectors and for those caught up in stupid choices, botched dreams and dreadful disappointments. Today Jesus comes for homeless people, executives, addicts, public servants, AIDS victims, rock stars, farmers, IRS agents, soldiers, hookers, athletes—for you and me. Jesus is clearly aware that this will provoke the condemnation of the religious elite. He challenges those who follow rules to achieve rightness with God. What an irony: Those who talk the most about others' need for a savior are often blind to their own need for one.

Jesus' response to the Pharisees in Matthew 9 should be read, reread and pondered until its words have worked their way into the fabric of our lives. Ever since Jesus came, every generation has attempted to dim the blinding brightness of its meaning. Brennan Manning observes:

> We think salvation belongs to the proper and pious, to those who stand at a safe distance from the back alleys of existence, clucking their judgments at those who have been

soiled by life. . . . In effect, Jesus says the Kingdom of his
Father is not a subdivision for the self-righteous nor for those
who feel they possess the state secret of their salvation. The
Kingdom is not an exclusive, well-trimmed suburb with
snobbish rules about who can live there. No, it is for a larger,
homelier, less self-conscious cast of people who understand
they are sinners because they have experienced the yaw and
pitch of moral struggle.

This means that we can finally stop lying to ourselves and de-
ceiving others. We can finally admit, without fear of reprisal,
shame or guilt, that despite knowing Jesus and being forgiven, the
fierce clash with lust, envy, fear and pride still rages inside us. We
can acknowledge that we are often unkind, mean, angry, selfish
and resentful, especially toward those we love. Yet we have been
warmly embraced and wildly welcomed into God's family. God,
whose very nature is love, will never love us any more or less because of what we fail to do. Therefore, we don't have to strive to
make ourselves acceptable to God. We can embrace our deficiency
and helplessness and failure, knowing we have been deeply and
irreversibly forgiven.

The person who understands the gospel can't avoid being lost
in the adoration, wonder and praise of the triune God. We don't
repent in order to earn forgiveness; we repent because we are forgiven. Repentance is an expression of our appreciation for what
has been freely given to us. The sequence of forgiveness and then
repentance, rather than repentance and then forgiveness, is crucial if we are to understand the scandalous gospel of God's grace.

The knowledge that our heavenly Father knows us completely
is a great relief for shame-filled and guilt-riddled people like me.
We no longer live in fear that some tattletale will blow the whis-
tle on us; no adversary can make an accusation against us stick;

no closet skeleton can expose our gruesome past; no character flaw can cause God to turn and run away from us. Our Father called us to himself in the full knowledge of everything that was against us.

A LOOSE CANNON ON THE PHARISEES' DECK

Filled with grace and truth, Jesus was far too dangerous for the Pharisees' comfort. To them his notion of grace was preposterously inclusive. How could Jesus dare and claim to be God? God would never be so careless about the people he associated with and called his friends! Jesus ate in the wrong neighborhoods, hung out with the wrong crowds and healed on the wrong day. *If he's been sent from God, why isn't he the same as us?* the Pharisees wondered.

Jesus was like a loose cannon on the Pharisees' deck, making grace far too abundant, too extreme, too scandalous and too outrageous. They insisted on a standardized regulatory system based on their interpretation of God's law. It consisted of principles, rules, proof texts, moral absolutes and *religious certainty.*

Religious systems strain to reduce God to a kind of mathematical equation that can be solved. Religious people are comforted when the mystery of God has been solved; this illusion empowers them with a precise understanding of how God functions. The religious want a domesticated, polite and manageable deity.

Mike Yaconelli understood and exposed this. His attraction to grace was boldly proclaimed in Youth Specialties' (the company Mike cofounded) statement of faith:

> Grace is outrageously unfair, ridiculously extravagant, and unashamedly the center of the gospel, and it sure beats judgmentalism, legalism, and all the other -isms. Grace always gives second chances, third chances, and never stops giving

chances. Grace has Jesus written all over it. Grace makes people nervous because they are always worried someone is going to take advantage of it. But that's what we like about grace. You *can* take advantage of it. But here's the interesting part—grace doesn't just let everyone in. Anyone, yes, but not everyone. And the Grace of God frequently includes the unexpected. So . . . who's in and who's not? Only God knows, and that's fine with us.

For Mike, these were not mere words. Mike was very serious about grace.

GRACE, WILD AND FREE

Mike was killed in a single-car crash on October 30, 2003. I attended his funeral in Yreka, California, with the "Notorious Sinners" (see p. 95). Whether he knew it or not, Mike helped me find my place among this group of men. I thank God for Mike's insistence that I "get real" with him and own the fact that my life too is a mess.

"Hopelessly flawed and hopelessly forgiven." These were the words on my mind as I approached the plain pine coffin containing Mike's body. Responding to the unusual invitation to personally express our thoughts and prayers with a magic marker, I penned these words on the side of his coffin: "Mike Yaconelli, hopelessly flawed and hopelessly forgiven . . . Yet, messy no more."

My trip home was flooded with personal memories of Mike and with the stories his family and friends had told. I reflected on the ways grief had affected my life in the past and wondered how it would this time around. I was acutely aware of how my relationship with Mike was one of a kind.

For the remainder of the winter and throughout the spring, my grief ran a common course. Grief and gratitude for my friendship with Mike unfolded side by side. However, as summer approached, bringing with it the annual gathering of the "Notorious Sinners," I began noticing something unusual. At random times throughout the day a profound sadness would sweep over me. So I began asking God, "Please, if there's something you're trying to tell me, don't let me overlook hearing it."

Within days, my typically peaceful sleep was interrupted by a recurring nightmare. Rarely able to recall my dreams, I was deeply troubled yet cautiously curious too. Each time the nightmare repeated itself, I was standing among an enormous mass of people (it felt like all the people of the world) tightly squeezed together on a shoreline. It was eerily dark and damp and cold. Suddenly, an imposing voice explained that in moments we were all going to begin swimming "for a shore beyond sight." Immediately there was a cacophony of anxious questions, angry protests and desperate pleas. I could feel a blanket of hopelessness and terror falling across the entire crowd. Though most people feared for their life, a confident few seemed certain of their ability to survive. They also appeared blind to the hopeless terror of the others.

Can this really be happening? I recall thinking. Within moments, I was moving with the throng into the water. It was the most awful, horrifying and hopeless circumstance I'd ever experienced. Every imaginable type of person was surrounding me: young and old, poor and rich, humble and proud, wise and foolish, strong and weak, able-bodied and challenged. A raging conflict swelled within me as I struggled to discern whether to aid others or to struggle for my own survival.

Hours of agony unfolded as I witnessed countless people drown and I depleted nearly all of my resources in the battle to save my own hide. Slowly, I began confronting the reality of my own impending death. After all hope had dissipated, I heard something in the distance. I stopped all my movement and heard someone whistling a light-hearted tune. There was also the sound of laughter. *Could this be the aquatic equivalent to a mirage in a desert?* I wondered. Energized by these hopeful sounds, I was given new energy to swim toward the sounds. As they grew louder and more distinct, I felt confident they must be real.

My first sighting was of a multicolored umbrella hat sometimes seen at the pool, the beach or a ballgame. Swimming toward the person with the hat, I realized it was Mike Yaconelli! He was floating on his back, laughing and occasionally batting one of many beach balls flying through the air. Surrounding him was a band of people who had, as it were, gathered on the sidelines, while countless others struggled to save their life. Mike's eyes met mine and the grin on his face diminished; he grew sad. As I swam to his side, he began shaking his head in apparent disbelief. *Dude*, he said, *What in the —ll are you doing?*

Immediately, I was overwhelmed with feelings of outrage and confusion. I screamed my response, "What do you think I'm doing, Mike? I'm trying to save my life!"

Still shaking his head, Mike spoke again. His tone was gracious and marked by compassion. "Brother, you don't get it, do you? Fil, can't you understand? There's no way for you to make it! None of these people can. Not a single one."

I shouted back in anger: "So, Mike, what's the point? Just give up! Is that what you expect me to do? Since I'm going to die anyway, I guess you're going to invite me to join your meaningless party."

He appeared unscathed by my outburst. Peering into my eyes with deep compassion and amazing care, Mike spoke again. "Fil, you don't have to die. You don't have to strive to achieve what is impossibly beyond your reach. Don't you understand? All you have to do is wait! He's coming to get us. I know he'll keep his promise. Jesus is coming to get us!"

That was it! God was reminding me of a great truth. It was the very thing that Mike's life had reflected: an unflinching confidence in the outrageous grace of God. Although Mike attempted to clean up his act and succeed in being faithful, he knew that he'd never get it right. Mike lived peacefully, knowing that he was hopelessly flawed and hopelessly forgiven.

My life will never be the same. He demonstrated that following Jesus is anything but neat and tidy. Far from it! Life with Jesus is complicated and perplexing—and I've begun to make peace with the disorderly, sloppy, chaotic look of my life as I'm giving him more and more of my heart.

THE LION IS GOD

One of the most profound and thought-provoking books I've read is *Christianity Rediscovered*. It was written by Vincent Donovan, a Roman Catholic priest. Superficially it's a good story about how one man lived among the Masai people in Tanzania and eventually brought them to Christian faith, yet it's something much more than that. It recounts his soul's journey, a disconcerting, shattering, humbling journey, but also one of discovery and freedom. On this journey Donovan rediscovered Christianity as well as the tasks of Jesus' followers.

Donovan began his life among the Masai in 1965. Within a year he was questioning long-established missionary practices. Troubled by the lack of impact on people's lives, he surmised that the gospel message expressed no power and vibrancy. Eventually he began doubting Christianity's validity for the Masai and himself. Calling this season in his life a "crisis of faith," he contemplated calling it quits. As his faith continued in a downward spiral Donovan experienced a "shattering" that caused him bodily pain.

Months after the crisis ended, Donovan was sitting with a Masai elder discussing the anguish of belief and unbelief. The elder explained that the Masai word Donovan was using for "faith" was not sufficient. It meant literally "to agree to." Of course Donovan had known the word had that shortcoming, but it was the closest possible word for him to use. The elder said this kind of belief was similar to a hunter shooting an animal from a great distance: only his eyes and finger would take part in the act.

The elder insisted that another word must be found to accurately communicate what it means to be in intimate union with God. He expressed that to believe is like a lion stalking its prey, as its nose, eyes and ears pick up its scent and the sounds of the prey's movement. The lion's leg strength gives it the speed to catch its victim. When the lion is strategically positioned, it then uses all the power of its upper body to pounce on it. The elder described this as "the terrible death leap," the moment when a single blow to the neck kills the prey. As the animal goes down, the lion envelopes it in his arms, pulling it to him and making it part of himself. "A lion kills this way," the elder explained. This is also how a person believes. *This* is what comprises intimate union with God.

Silenced by the elder's provocative depiction, Donovan sat in amazement. Donovan now fully grasped that this kind of union with God explained why his body ached from head to toe when his intimate connection to God was seemingly lost. Nonetheless, Donovan's wise old teacher was not yet finished.

Donovan recalled the elder's final remarks:

> "We did not search you out, Padri," he said to me. "We did not even want you to come to us. You searched us out. You followed us away from your house into the bush, into the plains, into the steppes where our cattle are, into the hills where we take our cattle for water, into our villages, into our homes. You told us of a High God; how we must search for

him, even leave our land and our people to find him. But we have not done this. We have not left our land. We have not searched for him. He has searched for us. He has searched us out and found us. All the time we think we are the lion. In the end, the lion is God."

PAUSE AND PONDER

- What has more often than not been the controlling force in your life with God: *rules* or *relationships?*

- How do you respond to Jesus' questions: "Are you tired? Worn out? Burned out on religion?"

- Have you learned from Jesus "the unforced rhythms of grace"?

6 Worse Than Blindness

"A blind man knows he cannot see, and is glad to be led, though by a dog; but he that is blind in his understanding, which is the worst blindness of all, believes he sees as the best, and scorns a guide."

SAMUEL BUTLER

It was a hot, muggy summer afternoon, and a steady rain had been falling for days. I was a middle schooler, and I was hanging out at my best friend Mark's home. As I lazily sauntered through the den, his dad, Charlie, obviously spellbound, was standing by the sliding glass door overlooking their soggy back-yard. When he realized that I had entered the room, he shouted, "This is utterly amazing. I cannot believe what I'm seeing. Fil, you have got to take a look at this. Hurry, before they're gone. Just look at all those frogs. I've never seen anything like this in my entire life."

I joined him by the door and began searching for the frogs. *What in the world is he talking about? This guy has gone crazy*, I remember thinking. *I don't see any frogs.* Yet, despite my inability to see them, Charlie was actually seeing frogs. There must have been a hundred of them.

It didn't take us long to figure out the difference between Mark's dad and me. Because Charlie was colorblind, he was able to see things that I couldn't. Determined to prove that he wasn't crazy, he opened the back door so I could hear their croaking, and then rushed to retrieve a pair of polarized sunglasses. When I put on the sunglasses, I was finally able to see the frogs.

Although Charlie was able to see frogs and I couldn't, he was the one I inwardly labeled *blind!* Though I initially believed he was crazy, I was the one who couldn't see.

AN EXTRAORDINARILY UNIQUE WAY OF SEEING

Jesus understands our natural condition. We don't naturally see; we have to be taught how to see. On the other hand, Jesus has a unique way of seeing all things, and like Charlie, Jesus wants us to see the things as he sees them. Jesus especially wants us to see that nothing is more dangerous than blind people who are certain they see clearly. Intimate connection with God is most easily missed by arrogantly supposing that we've got God in our pocket and we possess all the answers to the mystery of faith. But until we see as Jesus does, we'll never see anything clearly.

The dark condition of the world is brilliantly reflected in the words of Isaiah.

> The people who walked in darkness
>   have seen a great light;
> those who lived in a land of deep darkness—
>   on them light has shined. (Isaiah 9:2 NRSV)

Isaiah's depiction is as precise and rich with meaning today as it was centuries ago. We live in a world where nobody can naturally see clearly. Living in this dark world causes us to sometimes feel a sense of doubt, of being lost, of being scared. In the darkness conflict is born between races, nations, genders, political parties, faith traditions and individuals. This darkness, which permeates our world, is seen in our newspapers, music, movies, literature, work, churches and relationships.

I've certainly experienced my share of darkness. There have

been days when I've been as disoriented and confused as the cartoon character Charlie Brown, who ambles up to Lucy's five-cent psychology booth for some guidance about life.

Lucy explains to him that life is like a deck chair on a cruise ship. Some people face their chair so that they can see where they have been. Other people put their deck chair right up on the bow of the ship so they can see where they are going.

Having provided her perspective on life, Lucy looks at her forlorn client and asks, "Which way is your deck chair facing?"

Without a moment of hesitation, Charlie replies dolefully, "I can't even get my deck chair unfolded."

Charlie Brown and I are two of a kind.

Everywhere I turn, there are people with answers—preachers, teachers, authors, experts, family members and friends—who are eager to explain God's plan for the best placement of my deck chair, but I've somehow spent most of my life in the darkness unable to unfold it. The truth is, I have fewer answers today than ever before. Yet I also have greater faith. I seem to be getting smaller as God gets larger, and that feels like a good thing.

Because darkness has crept into each of our lives, we can be assured that our vision will be distorted. One of the most critical effects will likely be on our prayer. As I travel, speaking at conferences and directing retreats, I've observed that darkness is one of a few dominant issues confronted by those who pray routinely. Among those who don't routinely pray, some issue related to darkness is often one of the causes.

Apparently this universal darkness was foremost in Jesus' mind on the day he returned to his hometown synagogue. His mission was to expose the deadly nature of spiritual blindness and reveal that he alone had the cure. As everyone gathered, Jesus, embodying the "great light" Isaiah spoke of, stood and read the prophet's words,

The Spirit of the Lord is upon me,
>   because he has anointed me
>   to bring good news to the poor.
> He has sent me to proclaim release to the captives
>   and recovery of sight to the blind,
>   to let the oppressed go free,
> to proclaim the year of the Lord's favor.

After he was seated he declared, "Today this scripture has been fulfilled in your hearing" (Luke 4:18-19, 21 NRSV).

JESUS OUR LIBERATOR

Jesus came to enrich our impoverished lives with the good news that we are of infinite value. With unrivaled kindness and mercy, Jesus our liberator comes crashing into our life declaring that we don't have to struggle any longer to get God to recognize and affirm us. He's come to liberate us from the "merit badge" mentality that religion promotes and to restore our vision and rid us of the notion that we're in the middle of a cosmic game of crime and punishment. He's here to put an end to the oppression religion imposes. He's come to dispel the myth that we get what we deserve and strive hard to attain. He's here to help us experience the radical nature of his grace.

In a nutshell, Jesus came to help us see *how* and *why* religion is bad. Listen to his portrayal of the purveyors of religion.

> They talk a good line, but they don't live it. They don't take it into their hearts and live it out in their behavior. It's all spit-and-polish veneer.
>
> Instead of giving you God's Law as food and drink by which you can banquet on God, they package it in bundles of rules, loading you down like pack animals. They seem to take pleasure in watching you stagger under these loads, and wouldn't think of lifting a finger to help. (Matthew 23:3-4)

Their outlook made God into a harsh and demanding slave owner, and the law became God's whip and our shackles. Unlike Jesus, who focused on the center of a person's life, the religious focus on the boundary markers—the highly visible and superficial practices that make it easy to determine who is "in" and who is "out."

The following questions are intended to assist you in discerning whether you're living in bondage to religion or in intimate union with God. Ponder your response to each one. And feel free to be truthful, at least with your self.

- Does your life with God lift you up or drag you down?

- Does thinking about God generate joy and lightheartedness or depression and heaviness?

- Does God's presence in your life help and encourage or hurt and haunt you?

- Are you becoming more or less gracious, loving and approachable?

- Are you becoming more or less judgmental, exclusive and proud?

- Has your awareness of God's relentless love and care been heightened and drawn you more deeply into an intimate connection with God?

Whenever our relationship with God becomes a depressing affair, manufacturing a supply line of burdens and prohibitions while insisting that we constantly respond to an endless parade of oughts, it is in all likelihood a relationship with religion instead.

FANATICAL BLINDNESS

Jesus hit the nail on the head on numerous occasions, shocking the Pharisees with the news that they were spiritually blind. Regrettably, many of us are afflicted with their malady, and like them we can't see it. Religion has a way of blinding us to the truth that we are God's beloved sons and daughters. Instead, it teaches us to believe that striving to be moral is our only hope. Religion stuffs us with knowledge about God that fails to intersect our life with God's. Religion leads us into the deadly illusion that our lives are full and complete, creating an arrogance that insulates us from needed correction and authentic growth. Religion makes us blind followers of religion who believe we're following Jesus.

Jesus enables us to see that God does not desire saying right words, thinking pure thoughts or doing good deeds. His primary concern is our relationship with him.

> God made the world and everything in it. He is Lord of heaven and earth, and he doesn't live in temples built by human hands. He doesn't need help from anyone. He gives life, breath, and everything else to all people. From one person God made all nations who live on earth, and he decided when and where every nation would be.
>
> God has done all this, so that we will look for him and reach out and find him. He isn't far from any of us, and he gives us the power to live, to move, and to be who we are. "We are his children." (Acts 17:24-28 CEV)

Recently I attended a very intense college football game. Leaving the stadium I was also convinced that it was the most poorly officiated game I'd ever seen. As a fan exiting alongside me remarked, "Wow, that was quite a game. It's too bad the referees didn't see it!" However, that evening, taking advantage of modern technology, I watched the recorded telecast of the game. I was stunned and chastened to discover that the officiating appeared to be without error. I suspect that viewing the game from great distance with thirty-five thousand desperately hopeful fans longing for our team to pull out a victory had resulted in fanatical "blindness."

We all have undetected blind spots. Once we suffer religion's stain, our spiritual vision plays tricks on us, and despite being blind we are certain we see clearly. We become like the elderly driver who insists that there's nothing wrong with his vision. Meanwhile, he poses a deadly threat to everyone he passes. Under religion's influence, we'll never see anyone clearly—not God, ourselves, our family, our friends, our colleagues or our enemies. Instead, we'll stumble in the dim shadows of prejudicial judgment, religious ritual, guilt, shame and emptiness. This is why Jesus remains near, so he can guide us to see the things that we have not been willing or able to see.

Yet, having Jesus near isn't always comfortable or easy. There are times when we would rather be left alone. At times the light Jesus shines into our lives is too revealing for our comfort. We would rather avoid or camouflage much of what we see in the light. Sometimes when we sense that Jesus is not looking, we may try to run from him and hide in places where we hope he'll not find us. However, he remains near, coaxing us to examine the dark shadows of our life.

Last week I sat with my family and watched a college basketball game representing one of the fiercest rivalries in sports. With 14.5 seconds left, one of the players went for a lay-up and was struck in the face by an opponent's right elbow. Blood poured from his nose and onto the court. I jumped from my chair and began cursing the offending player. Within moments I was embarrassed by my outburst, yet too proud to admit it. Later that night, after my family had gone to bed, I sat alone wallowing in shame and self-contempt. *Fil, you are such a jerk! Why do you imagine that you can know another person's motives? You disgust me.*

Despite Jesus' nearness and the restored vision he provides, I still find that I am amazingly adept at seeing the negative. Why is my vision still overshadowed by the pointing fingers and accusing voices? Why am I so often blind to the "high fives" of God's loving approval? Why does the specter of my unworthiness linger while the awareness of God's delight in me so quickly fades? When will my awareness of God's grace shatter the wall of inadequacy that surrounds my deaf and dumb heart?

To these and other similar questions the only certain answer I can give is: I don't know. However, I know that God is continuing to heal my blindness, and I'm beginning to see three things in particular that are making a drastic difference in my life.

Seeing Clearly with Jesus

Vision 1: The L.I.F.E. principle. Religion taught me to believe that the Christian life is cozy and predictable. I was told that if I faithfully follow Jesus, I'll experience a stable, whole and serene life. Therefore, whenever I felt isolated, lonely and cold, the problem was undoubtedly me.

This is not the kind of life God invites us into. Living in intimate union with God is radically different because with God "Life Is Fabulously Exciting" (L.I.F.E.). It's like a tandem bicycle ride on an up-and-down and twisted mountain trail. When our ride together first began, my religious training led me to imagine that my proper place was on the front seat steering the bike, while God was in the back helping me pedal. (That's why Mom always warned me when I was going out on a date, "Remember. God will be in the back seat.") As long as I was steering I always took the most direct, easiest and safest route.

When I decided it was time to break a few of my religion's rules, Jesus and I switched places, and it made all the difference in the world. Jesus had a different agenda that focused more on the journey and less on the destination. He seemed to take the long way,

up mountains and through rough and rocky places and at break-
neck speeds. At times it was all that I could do to hang on. Sometimes I worried and grew anxious and asked, "Where are you taking me?" More than once I screamed in terror, "Are you crazy?
You're going to get me killed!" But Jesus just laughed, and looking
back I realize that's when I started learning to trust.

And the most amazing thing is that I'm learning to show up and
shut up and pedal in the strangest places. I'm beginning to enjoy
the view and the cool breeze on my face as I journey with my incomparably delightful companion, Jesus. When I'm terrified, he
tells me, "Relax. Trust me." And when I'm sure I can't pedal any
more, he just smiles and says, "Pedal."

Thus Jesus is helping me see life differently. Now I'm conclud-
ing that the ups and downs, and successes and failures, will be my
constant companions. I'm seeing that life with Jesus is not about
life getting *better* as much as it is about life getting *different*. Instead of seeing how to qualify, quantify, evaluate, compare and
cope, I'm learning how to enjoy, embrace, endure, savor and hold
on for the ride of my life.

Vision 2: The lopsided principle. Religion projected a positive,
compelling image of how balanced my life would be if I vigilantly
followed all of its rules. Like a bronze statue of some famous and
brave warrior, my life would appear equally remarkable and heroic.

Thankfully, Jesus has enabled me to see there's no such thing as
a balanced life for those who are seriously following him. Oh,
there may be balance if we never get up from our padded church
pew to follow Jesus into some of the challenging places.

The issue in life is not precision and *balance*; it's *balancing*. Instead of trying to get all of my ducks in a row, I'm recognizing that
my life is supposed to be lopsided. What looks like balance in
someone else's life would spell disaster for me. Best of all, living by
this principle helps to keep me in constant communication *with*,

in utter reliance *on* and deeply grounded *in* Jesus.

Following Jesus is like walking on a tightrope. Distractions surround me, become my focal point and spell my doom. At any moment an unanticipated gust of wind blows and threatens to knock me off balance. Seemingly from out of nowhere a bird crosses my path. Far beneath me, among the many who have gathered to cheer me on, someone's jeer has the power to threaten my balancing act. To successfully accomplish my crossing, I must be continually *balancing*. How do we do this? Jesus is obviously the best one to ask.

Everything we know about Jesus indicates that he was concerned with one thing: doing the will of God. Nothing in the Gospels is as compelling as Jesus' single-minded devotion and obedience to his Father. From his first recorded words to his anxious parents in the temple, "Didn't you know that I had to be here, dealing with the things of my Father?" (Luke 2:49), to his last words on the cross, "Father, I place my life in your hands!" (Luke 23:46), Jesus' only concern was doing his Father's will. He says, "The Son can't independently do a thing, only what he sees the Father doing" (John 5:19).

This has become one of the most essential things about Jesus' life for me to observe and let sink in. Jesus is our Savior Immanuel not only because of what he said to us and did for us, but also because it was said and done in obedience to his Father. The distinction is enormous! It's why Paul wrote, "Here it is in a nutshell: Just as one person did it wrong and got us in all this trouble with sin and death, another person did it right and got us out of it. . . . One man said no to God and put many people in the wrong; one man said yes to God and put many in the right" (Romans 5:18-19). So, what's the big deal? What's my point? Simply this: The center of Jesus' life is his obedient relationship with God, and so it must become in our life.

Vision 3. The naming principle. Religion blinded me to yet another essential truth—about me! Religious training led me to conclude that I was a failure, no good and a disappointment to God—unless I could find a way to demonstrate the opposite. Looking to the world for a more hopeful basis of identity, I was informed that I am what I *have,* what I *do* and what others *say about me.* This led me into self-rejection's trap.

The most deadly trap in life is self-rejection. Although success, approval and power pose their own threats, their alluring quality often comes from the way they lead to the much larger and more deadly temptation of self-rejection. When we conclude that we are good-for-nothing and in some peculiar way unlovable, then success, approval and power are appealing solutions. However, the most fatal trap of all is self-rejection.

I am amazed at how quickly and how often I fall prey to this trap's lure. Immediately, upon hearing of someone's criticism or displeasure with me, I find myself thinking, *Well, there's further proof that I am a nobody, a total loser.* The power of one criticism has often proven to be far greater than a hundred approvals. A recent example occurred last weekend while I was speaking at a men's conference. I don't recall an occasion when I've received more public and private affirmation for my presentations. However, after the final session on Sunday afternoon a gentleman approached me and cut me off at the knees. "Your presentations were a tremendous disappointment to me this weekend. I wish I hadn't come." The weight of that one criticism proved to be far greater than all the praise I was given.

Perhaps you think that arrogance is a bigger problem than self-rejection. But isn't self-promotion just the other side of self-rejection? Doesn't our arrogance put us above others in order to avoid being seen as we see ourself? Bottom line, isn't arrogance simply another way of coping with feelings of worthlessness?

Painfully hidden beneath my arrogance lies enormous self-doubt, and a massive quantity of pride is hidden in my self-rejection. Therefore whether I'm inflated or deflated, I've lost sight of the truth and become blind to reality.

Self-rejection is the most formidable foe we face because it blinds us to the truth that God wants us to see regarding ourselves.

So, who does God say I am? What is the core truth of our existence?

Recently I've been riveted by the Gospels' report of Jesus' baptism: "And a voice came from heaven: 'You are my Son, whom I love; with you I am well pleased'" (Luke 3:22 NIV). I find God's timing most intriguing. How much more sensible and appropriate for the Father to affirm Jesus following the Sermon on the Mount or another extraordinary moment in Jesus' ministry. However he chose to declare his pleasure when Jesus had yet to preach a sermon or heal anyone! Clearly, God's love for us isn't contingent on our performance.

To see clearly, we must look continually for people and places where the truth is spoken and we are reminded of our deepest identity as beloved and chosen. Jesus assists me to see the essential value of these people and places. He helps me recognize that without them I remain blind to essential truths about myself. People who reveal these truths to us also name what we are unable to name—the positive ways we express our faith. I'm an expert at pointing out what I do wrong or could do better. I desperately need friends who can identify what I do well or good or right.

Can you relate to the things I'm describing? Has religion caused you to become your own worst enemy? Do you long to be set free from the shame and disappointment religion has forced on you? If so, there's good news coming!

The last time I saw my friend Mike Yaconelli was on October 27, 2003. We had just directed a retreat for a group of youth workers. After saying goodbye, I went to grab my belongings. As I ex-

ited the hotel I noticed Mike standing at a busy intersection waiting for the light to change. My first instinct was to speak with him
again. However, I hate goodbyes, so I chose instead to duck behind a column and observe him. (Mike intrigued me.) As a large
crowd from the conference began crossing the street, Mike appeared to be in a hurry. I wondered, *Is he afraid someone's going to
recognize him and want to talk? Or is he afraid no one is going to
recognize him and want to talk?* Three days later Mike was dead.

On Sunday, November 2, 2003, I listened as his son Mark reflected on his dad's life. He recounted a conversation Mike told
about concerning his spiritual director: "So then, out of the blue,
she asks me, 'Can you think of an image or symbol that represents
how you see yourself?' Bam! It came to me immediately. You know
that story I've told for fifteen years about the overweight, unattractive, lame girl that no one wants to dance with? That's me.
That's how I see myself! That's why I like that story so much! I'm
the unattractive lame girl!"

Mike was "beaming with insight like a five-year-old proudly
presenting his first self-portrait." Mark was shocked and confused:
"My dad, published author, successful businessman, pastor and
speaker-in-demand, was an undesirable, disabled, homely, heavy-
set junior high girl?"

I recalled watching Mike cross the street a few days earlier.

Mark continued, "Although this may sound like a cute insight
within a man who continually played with his own sense of identity and relationship with God, I've realized it's one of the keys to
understanding my dad's love for Jesus and the way he lived his
life." Mark was unlocking a portion of the mystery of his dad's life.
"It was rare to listen to Dad speak and not hear the person who felt
rejected, isolated and incompetent."

As Mark described how his dad had spent twenty-seven years
living in the average, inconveniently located town of Yreka, Califor-

nia, his insight deepened. "Yreka is not a romantic little village. It's not a resort town." Offering apologies to his fellow Yrekans, Mark continued. "Yreka is a town of lame junior high girls." Explaining that his dad spent most of his time caring for people in Yreka without ever asking for any compensation or recognition, he posed the question, why? "Because he knew the pain of being an outcast, because he himself felt unwanted, because in a strange way it was the one place he felt accepted and at home—because it was the one place where the gospel came to life, where his gifts were drawn out, the place where he could hear Jesus most clearly."

Mark acknowledged that he had often wondered why his dad took so many speaking engagements, answered e-mail from strangers and appeared so pleased when people he'd never met wanted to talk.

> Because when you feel ugly and unattractive, what a joy it is to be wanted—yet the power of his ministry was that he had encountered a power in Jesus Christ that revealed something exceedingly beautiful and eternal in the midst of his brokenness. Despite all the voices around and within him that named him ugly, he'd heard the one voice that called him by his true name, "Beloved." He'd felt Jesus single him out despite all that was rough and unfinished in him.

There is a way out of the unworthiness, out of the dark tunnel of defeat and shame that religion leads us into. Jesus wants to meet us in that darkness and lead us toward the light. But the journey is long and sometimes difficult. However, Jesus offers friendship along the way that is second to none.

YOU DON'T KNOW ME
From the opening chapter of John's Gospel, it's obvious that Jesus paid careful attention to others. This was especially true in the

story of Jesus' first encounter with Nathanael. When Jesus approached Nathanael, Jesus said, "There's a real Israelite, not a false bone in his body" (John 1:47).

Wow! How could a person not feel proud after hearing such an assessment of his or her character? For those of us who have spent most of our life striving for this kind of recognition, this may have been our most defining moment. Yet Nathanael, justifiably perplexed, questioned Jesus' insight, replying, "Where did you get that idea? You don't know me" (John 1:48).

Jesus' answer was straightforward and precise. "One day, long before Philip called you here, I saw you under the fig tree" (John 1:48).

What would it have been like to meet Jesus face to face? After just a few moments Nathanael was certain he had never met a person like Jesus, exclaiming, "Rabbi! You are the Son of God, the King of Israel!" (John 1:49).

Immediately, Jesus warned Nathanael that he was in for the ride of his life. "You've become a believer simply because I say I saw you one day sitting under the fig tree? You haven't seen anything yet! Before this is over you're going to see heaven open and God's angels descending to the Son of Man and ascending again" (John 1:50-51).

Though we often crave being known as we really are, we are also terrified by the thought of being exposed. We're not fools. We have witnessed others' (and our own) cruel, unforgiving treatment of people, which exposes their (our) hypocrisy and phoniness. We know that followers of religion sometimes kill their wounded after they fall. And we know that the hardest thing about seeing and being seen is having to respond to what has been exposed.

DO YOU REALLY WANT TO BE SEEN?

The story of Nathanael presents probing questions to those whose lives have been deformed by religion: Do we really want Jesus to tell us what he sees when he looks at our life? Do we honestly want him to tell us who we really are in his eyes? If we answer yes, our life will never be the same. God is going to open our spiritual eyes, and eventually we are going to see *ourself* as does Jesus—in a profoundly new way.

Jesus makes this clear: When we're *willing* to let God see us, even the parts of ourselves that we have kept hidden so well for so long that we have forgotten they exist, our spiritually blind eyes will open, enabling us to see *everything* about ourself more clearly.

But we will never come completely out of hiding unless we trust God totally. With all of the shameful and painful things we have hidden in our lives, the only eyes we can gaze into without shamefully looking away are the eyes of God. It seems magical, almost too good to be true, that God's eyes could be so intense yet so loving, so revealing yet so protecting, so piercing yet so caressing, so intense yet so intimate, so distant yet so inviting.

The only experience that rivals the terror and dread I felt when imagining being seen by God is when my seventh-grade physical education class was required to take public showers at the conclusion of gym class. I'll never forget the utter terror I felt undressing in front of my peers and being seen naked. But with time I became more comfortable once I knew it was safe.

Do you honestly trust God? Do you really believe that seeing you as you are, God still loves you with wild and reckless abandon? I sincerely hope so! After all, it's true! God knows you through and through. God sees all things—all that you are, all that you have been and ever hope to become. Every experience of your life is known to God: every image that you've ever seen, each touch, every sensation, and every word you've ever heard or spoken. Each idea, emotion and thought that's imprinted on your soul is known to God. God knows you better than any other person in your life. God knows you better than you know yourself. And because of who you are, in spite of what you are, God loves you. Your value to God has no boundaries or breaking point. God loves you up and down, through and through. Nothing and nobody can remove you from God's loving presence. This is the reality God wants you to live within.

Looking back on my life I'm confident that God's voice was always present, assuring me of what I couldn't assure myself: that I'm unconditionally loved. What a heinous irony that it was my preoccupation with my religious performance that kept me from being able to accept God's recognition and acceptance as the sole source of my identity. While God was telling me what I longed to hear, louder voices challenged me to prove that I was lovable, to demonstrate my worth and earn the recognition and approval I so deeply desired. Thus it was an act of sheer mercy and grace that finally enabled me to realize that intimate union with God comes not from striving after faith but from resting in the faithful one.

That soft and truthful voice that declares that I am loved has come to me in countless ways. My parents, wife, children, friends, mentors and even many strangers have echoed that voice in many tones. I've been loved and cared for by an endless number of people with much tenderness and affection. I've been guided and encouraged with tremendous gentleness and devotion. I've been inspired to keep going when I wanted to quit, and challenged to try again when I failed. I've been recognized and affirmed for certain successes, yet somehow all of these demonstrations of love and affection have not been sufficient to fully convince me that I am beloved. Hovering in the dark shadows lurks the haunting question: If all of these who offer me the blessed gift of their recognition and approval could really see me and know me at my core, would they still love me? That torturous question, rooted in the core of my being, has kept condemning me and forcing me to flee the very place where that soft voice calling me beloved could be heard.

Aren't we desperately hoping that some person, thing or event will occur, giving us that final feeling of peace and well-being we desire? Don't we sometimes hope that something or someone will become the fulfillment of our deepest desire? Of this I am convinced—as long as we are waiting for that inexplicable moment to occur, we'll go on running in restless and anxious confusion, always lustful and angry, never fully at peace or content. Take it from one who knows: this is the path to spiritual exhaustion and burnout, the wide road to spiritual death.

However, if we'll dare to believe Jesus, we can travel another road. We are his beloved, and were so long before our parents, teachers, spouses, children and friends loved or wounded us. This is the most fundamental truth of our lives.

LISTENING TO GOD'S VOICE

One of the most memorable events during Jesus' earthly life occurred on the Mount of Transfiguration (Luke 9:28-36). Jesus had taken Peter, James and John up a mountain to pray, and suddenly Moses, the great lawgiver, appeared with the prophet Elijah. As they discussed the Messiah's impending death and resurrection, Jesus, who was soon to become the fulfillment of both the law and prophecies, began radiating the Shekinah glory of God.

Peter jumped to the conclusion that this spectacular event called for decisive action. But as Peter began outlining his plan (Luke says that "he did not know what he was saying"), a cloud enveloped them and the voice of God declared, "This is my Son, my Chosen; listen to him!" (v. 35 NRSV).

Like Peter, I often feel the need to impulsively do something, to get busy, to try to make something happen. But I'm beginning to believe the voice of God, which says the most important thing is to be attentive to his presence, especially within my heart, and listen to him. When we don't take time to listen to that voice, we have no hope of awakening to and living out our true identity.

Communing with our Creator is an unrivaled and essential gift. When we listen to God and respond, our knowledge of God's relentless love moves from head to heart, where our spirit meets his Spirit. When we stop long enough to listen, we are bound to hear our true identity declared. In the stillness we come face to face with the living Lord, who knows us and loves us and says, "You are my beloved."

PAUSE AND PONDER

- How is darkness typically manifested in your life?

- Review your answers to the questions on page 129. Has this exercise helped you determine whether you're living in bondage to religion or in union with God?

- Ponder again the questions, Do you really want Jesus to tell you what he sees when he looks at your life? Do you honestly want him to tell you who you really are in his eyes?

7　Why This Waste?

"No act of kindness, no matter how small, is ever wasted."

AESOP

Attached to the top of my computer screen is a thin strip of paper with a simple saying. It fell from a fortune cookie near the end of my first dinner with our daughter Meredith and Gabe, the young man who became her husband. Being a sentimental sap, I may have kept it for that reason alone. However, the words are also significant. They convey one of the truest things about me: "You are a lover of words."

It's true. I am a lover of words. After all, words are important. Without them our lives lose meaning, and without meaning we cannot live. Words can offer understanding, perspective, vision and insight. Words can bring comfort, consolation, support and hope. Words can take away isolation, fear, shame and guilt. Words can bring personal freedom and profound gratitude, peace and joy. A word of love can be a supreme act of love. That's because when our words become flesh in our lives, the world is transformed.

Jesus is the living Word in the flesh. With Jesus, words and actions are one and the same. That's why he insists:

> Don't say anything you don't mean. . . . You only make things worse when you lay down a smoke screen of pious talk, saying, "I'll pray for you," and never doing it, or saying, "God be with you," and not meaning it. You don't make your words

true by embellishing them with religious lace. In making your speech sound more religious, it becomes less true. Just say "yes" and "no." When you manipulate words to get your own way, you go wrong. (Matthew 5:33-37)

A COMMON WORD LIKE *WASTE*

The English language, so I've been told, consists of more than 400,000 distinct words, most of which mean the same thing to me as they do to everybody else. For instance, people with even the most limited vocabulary understand that the common word *waste* means unwanted or undesired things. *Waste* is a general term, though there are many synonyms that have more specific meanings: *misapply, lavish, misuse, overdo, ravage, ruin, dissipate, desolate, ravage* and *destroy*. My favorites remain *squander* and *fritter away*.

My investment in meaningful relationships has not been a waste. Among the benefits and delights of a growing friendship are the knowledge, insight and wisdom that are passed on. Recently I've come to know someone whose particular gifts to me are the maxims he's learned along life's way. For example: "Nothing becomes dynamic until it becomes specific." The principle seems applicable when it comes to waste. I'm not overly concerned about waste until something I value is being wasted. My response becomes dynamic when the specifics involve something I value.

There's also a cultural dimension to the concept of waste. Wasting time, wasting money, wasting good food or being wasteful involve moral judgments that carry a great deal of weight in human interaction.

Here are some examples: my dad always smooths and reuses paper towels; chefs from some culinary traditions value cuts of meat that other chefs waste; parents may view a child's career in a rock band as a waste of their time and education (a judgment not shared by the child). Buying frivolous things or paying for disapproved pleasures wastes money.

I saw a T-shirt sporting this slogan: "I spent most of my money on beer, women, and cigarettes—the rest of it I just wasted." Another revealing illustration is the fact that Americans spend $20 billion each year on ice cream. In the meantime, according to the United Nations, over the next ten years it would take only $7 billion to provide clean water and basic sanitation for the entire world, and another $4 billion to finance basic health care that would prevent the death of three million infants each year.

Recently, I began cultivating a friendship with an Ethiopian studying in a local university. He's also a serious follower of Jesus, possessing a gentle spirit and a discerning eye. At the conclusion of his first year in the United States I asked him to sum up his observations of American life. He wasted no words in his assessment: "Too much." I asked him to be more specific. "Too much waste. Too much everything." When I asked him to elaborate even more, he said, "Christianity and greedy materialism appear one-and-the-same in America."

I believe my Ethiopian friend is right. Whether we like it or not, materialism is up and Christian spirituality is down. Materialism is a scandal among those of us who are followers of Jesus. In their book *Boiling Point: Monitoring Cultural Shifts in the 21st Century*, George Barna and Mark Hatch indicate that in our society the core values of Christians are very similar to those of non-Christians. Barna's research documents that the way evangelical Christians live reveals we don't believe what we profess. There's no way to deny that a sizeable portion of contemporary American Christianity has embraced a "gospel of wealth"—the pursuit of riches—while at the same time proclaiming believers should be concerned about the poor and oppressed.

A WASTE OF TALENT

Many people are devoid of interest in Jesus. For them, devotion and service to Jesus are foolish and a senseless frittering away of one's life. Jesus is a homeless, jobless, possessionless loser in their eyes.

Recently I read about an article in *Entertainment Weekly* concerning the death of Larry Norman, a talented Christian musician. Acknowledging the artist's devotion to Jesus, the writer called it a detriment to his career. "He really could've been a star if he were singing about something other than Jesus." In other words, "What a waste of talent!"

Shortly before his death, Norman dictated a message to a friend that offers a clue as to why he lived as he did. "I feel like a prize in a box of Cracker Jacks with God's hand reaching down to pick me up." Norman was so aware of Jesus' value to him and his value to Jesus that nothing else in his life mattered more.

I don't want to dwell too long on the attitude of those who view following Jesus as a waste. After all, it's to be expected. In contrast, most followers of Jesus (especially if they're like me) tend to care more about what *other followers* say about them. Sadly, I've often become more consumed with their opinion of me than Jesus' opinion.

For example, I recall the wounding remarks made by friends and family members regarding my career in youth ministry. Questions such as, When are you going to get a real job? and What will it take for you to realize you're wasting your time? were for years common and hurtful fare.

The endless battle with attachment to my reputation is mostly rooted in arrogance. When my life is rooted in the raging fury of the love of God, I'm free to accept the life that God has for me. His unique plan for me is more important than any human approval. Humility happens whenever Jesus' verdict regarding everything in my life annuls my own.

The apostle Peter says:

"God has had it with the proud,
But takes delight in just plain people."

So be content with who you are, and don't put on airs. God's strong hand is on you; he'll promote you at the right time. Live carefree before God; he is most careful with you. (1 Peter 5:5-7)

Allowing Peter's words to flow like streams of living water over my life and having them sink down into my soul has begun to produce authentic fruit.

THE TIMELESS CONUNDRUM

The Gospel of Mark exposes the difference between the things Jesus and his followers value and the values of those devoted more to religion. This disparity came into focus when a woman broke an alabaster jar of expensive perfume and anointed Jesus' head during a meal in Simon the Leper's home. While Jesus gratefully received her extravagant gift, others responded harshly. All they were able to see was a grievous waste.

The perfume could have been donated for the relief of the poor instead of being emptied over Jesus' head, they apparently thought. The voices are pragmatic, upright and moralistic. It's difficult to read the critics' words without hearing the contempt they held for the sort of woman who'd buy luxurious perfume in the first place, let alone drench an unrelated man in its overwhelming fragrance. How inappropriate. What bad taste!

Before we take sides, though, let's be honest with ourselves. Who among us is willing to blame the guys around the table for being upset? Certainly not those of us who provide mercy and advocacy for the poor, the homeless, AIDS victims, the imprisoned, and other marginalized individuals and groups. Surely not the social worker who's aware of the most desperate cases and can't help. Positively not the homeless single parent without any food or money to care for his or her precious children. What emotionally healthy person who serves the needy would dare blame the religious men around that table? If anyone would be outraged, certainly Jesus would be! Who could stomach such an act of lunacy, even criminal neglect, by this wasteful woman?

Yet, Jesus was not outraged by her gift. To the contrary, he was offended by her critics' callous attack. And with the "wasted" perfume trickling down his beard and robe, Jesus sprang to her defense. "Leave her alone. . . . Why are you bothering her? She has done a beautiful thing to me" (Mark 14:6 NIV).

It's easy for me to imagine what might have raced through the men's bewildered minds. *Now hold on just a minute, Jesus! Did you just refer to this foolish waste by another name? Did you say what I think you said? Did you call this obvious waste "a beautiful thing"?*

Before the curtain fell on that intense scene, Jesus elevated the significance of her action to perplexing prominence: "I tell you the truth, wherever the gospel is preached throughout the world, what she has done will also be told, in memory of her" (Mark 14:9 NIV).

I've prayerfully pondered this story for the past several years and am convinced that it reveals insights into Jesus' values that can transform our lives. Yet tragically, religion has taught us to insulate ourselves from the force of such words. Religion takes sacred words like these and dissects them with an objective, impersonal eye. Religion teaches how to skin, stuff and mount living words, and then place them on display as if they were a trophy. Religion diminishes sacred, life-altering words to insignificant information. In so doing, it domesticates the voice of God and diminishes his words for our own convenience. Talk about waste!

We prefer a domesticated god, and so we pare God down to a more manageable, self-serving size. The trivialization of God has been *the* temptation, *the* preoccupation and *the* failure for religious people of all eras.

So we dispassionately talk about the woman and the perfume. It poses no threat to discuss her identity and speculate on why she offered her extravagant, perhaps wasteful, gift. We take no risk in silencing her harsh critics. And we facilely speculate about Jesus' defense of the woman. It's a brilliant strategy because we don't have to talk about ourselves. But it's also deadly.

Let's not be foolish. As we consider the implications of this story, let's be alert to the power of each word. Let's open ourselves to what it's saying to and about us. If we allow it, this story can become a mirror in which to see ourselves more clearly. It has the capacity to grab ahold of us and never let us go.

After all, God *is* speaking here; there's no historical distance from us. When we put ourselves inside the story, it's not a mere religious exercise. We must refuse the temptation to read it from a safe distance. We must dare to enter the story and take the woman's identity. We must also recognize ourselves among her critics. And if we're unable or unwilling to do so, we must ask why.

HOUSTON, WE HAVE A PROBLEM

Perhaps you remember the tag line "Houston, we have a problem" for the 1995 film *Apollo 13*. Flight commander James Lovell used this phrase (or one close to it) to report a life-threatening problem back to their Houston base. These days it continues to be used, often humorously, to report any type of problem.

Like the Apollo 13 astronauts, those of us who follow religion more closely than we follow Jesus have a problem. And ours, like that of the astronauts, is also life-threatening. Our crisis has to do with what we value most and the consequences of those values. Like those who believed the gift of perfume was a waste, some of us have adopted religious values that place *usefulness* above *service*.

Mark's story clearly reflects Jesus' priorities, highlighting that the world's needs were not preeminent to Jesus. Jesus wants us to be engaged and caring; he forbids indifference to the needs of others. He even goes as far as to say that when we care for the least, we're doing it to him. Nonetheless, he is the first priority.

By graciously accepting the woman's extravagant gift, Jesus left no room for doubt. Above all, Jesus must be the focal point of our affection and devotion. He makes it clear that we're to withhold nothing; indeed, we're to lavish upon him all that we have, even our very selves. Furthermore, if that is all he ever allows us to do, then that is certainly enough. There must never be any issue, need, opportunity, cause or crisis that takes precedence over him.

Therefore, the first question is never whether the poor have been fed, the rules have been kept or all other vitally important things have been accomplished. The first question is, have I given all of myself and whatever I possess (or possesses me) to Jesus?

We live in a world of immense and overwhelming human needs. So it's easy for these concerns to dominate our attention, especially when religion seduces us into thinking that if we do enough "good" things and resist enough "bad" things, God will be obligated to accept us. Yet Jesus is not interested in our usefulness.

Following Jesus consists of an unconditional friendship, which naturally leads to selfless service to others. But our friendship with Jesus cannot be measured by our usefulness or fruitfulness. The Lord's first concern is our intimacy and openness with him. Whatever is our alabaster jar—our most prized possession, the dearest thing in the world to us—we must give to the Lord.

To some, especially the religious, that act will appear a waste, but that is what he requires more than any other thing. Often, our gift will be found in tireless and endless service, but Jesus reserves the right to suspend our service in order to help us know what our greatest affection is.

A REMARKABLE STORY

Over forty years ago I heard a remarkable story that continues to profoundly affect my life. The values of a renowned Christian servant illustrate the values Jesus intends his followers to embrace. The story is so remarkable that I've sometimes wondered whether it's true. Yet I've never doubted that it could be true. More importantly, I've longed for the same clarity of purpose and devotion in my life.

"Years ago," the storyteller began, "when I learned this person was speaking at an event in the city where I lived, I was determined to meet him. I yearned to understand the key to his devotion to Jesus and service to others. Locating the hotel where he was staying, I coaxed the front-desk attendant to give me his room number. Arriving at the door, I noticed that it was ajar, and just before knocking, I heard the person's voice. Not wanting to interrupt an important conversation, I moved closer and listened intently. What I heard I'll never forget. It was apparent he was alone and praying. Peering through the slight opening, I saw the person outstretched on the floor. The tone of his voice was that of someone begging.

"'Jesus, you know how much I value my friends and colleagues. Although I cherish their companionship and camaraderie, I could live without them, so I offer them back to you.

"'Thank you Jesus for honoring me by trusting me with opportunities to serve you and others. Yet, as much as I cherish the privilege of endeavoring to do these things for you, I could live without these opportunities. Therefore, I offer them to you.'

"His praying was earnest and heartfelt," the storyteller explained. "I began to suspect that this litany must represent everything he possessed, enjoyed and held dear. It also reflected the enormous challenges that had been woven into the fabric of his life. I eventually wondered where and how the prayer would end."

"'God, countless times I've expressed how grateful I am for my family. I know you understand better than anyone how difficult it is to let go of someone you love. God, I can't adequately thank you for my wife and children, yet I even could live without them. Therefore, today I release them again to you.'

"It was the rawest, most vulnerable, and relentlessly trusting prayer I'd ever heard," admitted the storyteller.

"'Abba, Jesus, Holy Spirit—I beg you. Whatever you choose, the one thing for which I plead is this: Please don't ever leave me alone. Take all of these cherished people, privileges and opportunities from me. But please, I beg you, don't ever, ever take yourself from me. You are above all things and the one person in my life that I cannot live without.'"

The storyteller, recalling again why he'd felt the compulsion to seek out this person originally, ended the story by declaring, "I never knocked. Instead I walked away grateful for the palpable answer that had been given me."

AN ENORMOUS, RADICAL SHIFT

This story coupled with the simple account of the woman anointing Jesus with perfume has generated a slow but certain shift, an enormous, radical movement, in my life. Jesus is ever more becoming the primary object of my affection. Let me emphasize that this is a seismic shift, away from my preoccupation with religion to an intimate relationship with an incomparably amazing Person.

For most of my adult life I've believed that nothing was more important than delivering the good news that God is in love with every person in the world. And through his sacrificial death Jesus has earned for us what we could never earn for ourselves; God has provided unconditional forgiveness for all of his creation.

However, pondering the mystery in Jesus' declaration "I tell you the truth, wherever the gospel is preached throughout the world, what she has done will also be told, in memory of her" (Mark 14:9 NIV) has caused a deep shift inside me. The gospel is meant to produce in me, just as it did in that woman, an unedited and unbridled response to Jesus.

THE GOSPEL TRUTH: YOU ARE LOVED!

This is the gospel truth: You are loved! God not only loves the world, God loves you. That's right, the God of the universe, the God of all creation, the God who created you and knows you by name, really and truly loves you! *Did you hear what I just said?* God is crazy about you!

How does knowing that you are profoundly loved make you want to respond? When you hear God say, "I have always loved you and I always will," what effect does it have on you? When God declares that you are unconditionally accepted, and then promises to give you mercy, grace, peace, love, kindness and faithfulness, how does that make you feel?

Jesus expresses that he loves you and urges you to make yourself at home in his love, and reminds you that the only reason you're able to love him is because he loved you first. Jesus will never forget you because he's got your name carved onto the palm of his hand as a constant reminder of his love for you.

You have a place in the heart of the most joyful, tenderhearted, kind and powerful person. And the same God who is crazy about you is also sovereign over all things. There is nothing in this world or beyond (death, life, angels, demons, the present, the future, powers, height, depth, not a single thing) that will ever be able to separate you from the love of God. Do these truths move you to praise him?

When both of your feet are planted firmly in the ground of God's love for you, and you're bathed in Christ's extravagant love, experiencing its breadth and length and depth and height, what difference does it make? During those remarkable moments when you suddenly know beyond a shadow of doubt that the Lord is with you, the God who takes unspeakable delight in you and rejoices over you with singing, does it change your disposition?

When your present and future, your health and destiny, your life and even your death depend totally on the God who sacrificed his only Son for weak, twisted and deceitful people like you and me, people with whom he's hopelessly in love, aren't you more joyful, grateful and free?

Is there any reason to worry about wasting everything on our gracious and loving God?

The Most Important Thing

When we are thinking about God, whatever comes into our mind is the most important thing about us. More than any other force, our concept of God is constantly giving our life its purpose, definition and meaning. When our thinking about God is correct, consistent and focused, we have the basis for thinking correctly about everything. However, when our thinking about God is incorrect, inconsistent or disjointed, we are thinking incorrectly about everything else in our life.

In his splendid book *God First Loved Us*, Antony Campbell observes:

> Originally, I believed the acceptance of a loving God involved a sufficient but relatively minor shift of attitude. After all, it was on so many people's lips. The more I worked with it, the more I realized that the acceptance in faith of God's unconditional love was not only hugely significant, it required a major change of attitude. . . . [T]he most major shift may be in the images we have of God and of ourselves. How radically is our image of God reshaped if we take seriously belief

in God as deeply, passionately, and unconditionally loving us? How radically must we rework our own self-image if we accept ourselves as lovable—as deeply, passionately, and unconditionally loved by God?

I'm convinced that the thing Jesus wants from us, more than any other thing, is our daily, unedited and unbridled response to God's unconditional love. That, I believe, is the most essential product of the gospel in our lives. The gospel is not just for sinners who have never heard or yielded to it. It's also for the rest of us whose foremost concern is how Jesus is shaping our everyday life, and how by enduring the disappointments and conflicts we can increasingly conform to the image of Jesus. The gospel is an ongoing, everyday matter. Every conflict, every disappointment, every hurt, every criticism challenges me to yield my hurt ego to Jesus as I continue to follow him.

MARKING THE MILESTONE

A few years ago, as Lucie and I approached our thirtieth anniversary, I pondered for weeks what would be an appropriate gift to mark the milestone. Although I'd successfully managed to project a glittering image of myself to others during those years, I'd failed her countless times. More than any other person, Lucie has faithfully endured the storms caused by my sometimes demanding, demeaning and hateful behavior. She has been witness to some of my darkest and most shameful moments. Numerous times I've given her justifiable cause to withhold her love or even walk away from our marriage. Instead, she has faithfully remained with me as a constant and dazzling expression of the unconditional love, devotion and faithfulness of Jesus to me.

Therefore I wanted to present her with something more exceptional than any gift I'd ever given to her. Oddly, what kept coming to my mind was jewelry. This was odd for one simple reason: I hate jewelry, mostly because I believe that it's frivolous, a waste. As our anniversary date drew nearer, I thought of the petite, inexpensive diamond ring I'd scrounged up enough money to purchase for her over thirty years ago. I couldn't seem to escape wondering how special she'd feel if I presented her with a new diamond ring. Yet, instinctively I reasoned, *Have you grown soft in the head? What are you thinking? Are you an idiot? You hate jewelry! Jewelry is a waste!*

Reflecting back, I'm confident that I've never given a gift, at least one that can be purchased, that had more meaning and significance than the diamond ring that she's proudly worn since June 5, 2006. She's fully aware that to me a gift of jewelry seems a waste. Yet I know that to her the ring I gave her is a beautiful thing. And we both know that my gift was given from a heart filled with undying devotion, gratitude and love.

WHAT DOES JESUS WANT?

I've discovered that my marriage and my relationship with Jesus have some things in common. If I'm unwilling to do certain things for the ones I cherish, things that they cherish, no great thing is going to happen in our relationship. Intimate friendship within the boundary of reason is a maimed friendship. Calculated love is no love at all. Although to me jewelry seems to be a waste, my wife likes jewelry. Similarly, when considering my relationship with Jesus, the question is plain and simple: Jesus, what do you want?

The biggest "diamond" Jesus wants is my attention. He wants me to be mindful of him during the unfolding moments of each day. Jesus wants me to become more alert and responsive to what he's saying. "This is the day the LORD has made," says Psalm 118:24. "Let us rejoice and be glad in it" (NIV). Some days the best I can manage is to weep or be angry or depressed, and to Jesus I think that's okay. Regardless of my state of mind, Jesus wants me to know that God is with me in each moment of each day.

Stop and think for a moment about *this* day. There has never been and will never be another day like it. This day is a remarkable day. If we were aware of how prized each day is, I suspect we'd hardly know how to live through it. Yet until we become aware of how valuable today is, we can't reasonably hope to be living at all.

"Oh, earth, you're too wonderful for anybody to realize you," said Emily in *Our Town*, Thornton Wilder's renowned play. Then she asked, "Do any human beings ever realize life while they live it? Every, every minute?"

"No," said the stage manager. "The saints and poets, maybe— they do some."

Sadly, it's not until Emily dies that she's able to look back on her life and then recognize the tragedy of small splendors lost each day as we anxiously and hurriedly scurry to and fro "so fast. We don't have time to look at one another."

Whether or not we're listening, I'm convinced that each day God woos us into the wasteful empty space of silent time alone with him. He does this so we'll recognize his presence throughout the day. Often, when I choose to join God in those quiet spaces, I discover some very disturbing things about myself, not the least of which is that I'm afraid to stop and listen. I fear what God might say or do *in* or *with* or *through* my life. Yet I also fear that I'll hear nothing at all. Another aspect of my fear is a byproduct of my religious training: my *activity* gives me significance and value in God's eyes, therefore I must never cease striving. I must remain busy.

Making space for God, which is wasteful, requires a willingness to not be in control. It requires opening myself in trust to the Holy Spirit. When I've been willing to offer this gift to God, I've slowly begun to see myself in a new and deeper way. Accepting the reality of my powerlessness and lack of control, I see more clearly my helplessness to solve my own or other people's problems or to change my little corner of the world. When I don't avoid or ignore the call into the empty space with God but choose to live in it, I discover a little bit more of the truth that the endless number of projects, plans, responsibilities and pressures that normally stalk me day and night become less urgent, and their grip on me is loosened. In a nutshell, I become more present, open and free.

Recently I went away on a personal retreat. Although I'd love to tell you otherwise, it wasn't spectacular. Like lots of personal retreats it seemed dreadfully uneventful. More apparent than any signs of God's presence were my own feelings of frustration, restlessness, boredom, sleepiness and uncertainty. Yet over time I've grown to believe that even when my time alone with God doesn't seem productive, more is happening than I recognize. Somehow my awareness that God loves me is increasing. Although I can't see his face or hear his voice, my awareness of God's nearness is increasing and my level of confidence in my ability to distinguish God's voice is increasing. The most telling sign to me that something important occurs during these retreats is in my sincere desire to return to these seemingly "wasted" times. Certainly there are exceptions, brought on by an endless list of things that get in the way. The weapons of mass distraction and self-destruction pose a constant threat. But the inner pull to return again is increasing, and I know that I must resist the conflicting urge to remain away.

THE SEEMINGLY WASTEFUL NATURE OF GOD
My grave concern for the evangelical community is our ever-increasing disregard for the seemingly extravagant, even wasteful nature of God. Meanwhile I fear that we're inching our way toward becoming a functional religion that insists on a rational purpose for everything. Thus we wind up taking ourselves more seri-

ously than we take God and measuring our worth as we imagine God does: by what we achieve. Whether consciously or unaware, we're suppressing the persistent wooing of the Holy Spirit, whose ancient reputation is associated with bypassing reason to arrive at redemptive wastefulness.

The gospel of Jesus Christ rescues us from the dizzying merry-go-round that religion forces us to ride. And while our head's still spinning, he tells us that it's okay to simply be ourselves and live freely. Jesus urges us to lose every trace of concern about failure and to jettison our pride over success. In other words, Jesus tenderly tells us to lighten up and to lighten our load. Meanwhile he makes the religious overachiever's blood boil by indicating his preference for those who have nothing to brag about and no achievements to lean on, for down-and-out sinners and the poor, the despised and dispossessed, those who are sick and for young children.

Mark recounts a scene that gets to the heart of the matter:

> The people brought children to Jesus, hoping he might touch them. The disciples shooed them off. But Jesus was irate and let them know it: "Don't push these children away. Don't ever get between them and me. These children are at the very center of life in the kingdom. Mark this: Unless you accept God's kingdom in the simplicity of a child, you'll never get in." Then, gathering the children up in his arms, he laid his hands of blessing on them. (Mark 10:13-16)

The disciples thought that children would distract Jesus from some important work he had to achieve. Playing with children is a waste of time. But Jesus sees things differently and lets the disciples know that he's furious. Whenever Jesus becomes angry, he exposes the absurd attitude of those he's annoyed with. Aware of the debate among the religious elite about whether children have a place in the kingdom, since they have no good deeds to show, Jesus uses children to illustrate how we all stand with God. No one is given a place in God's family because of what they achieve. Only by becoming small and childlike can we embrace the truth that we always stand before God empty-handed.

Making room for God and belonging to his family requires becoming completely ourselves, setting aside the roles and achievements we think will make us acceptable to God. For those who are proud of their achievements, this may be difficult, perhaps a pill that's too bitter to swallow.

Jesus takes time for the children and in so doing sets an improbable example. He doesn't teach them, because there's nothing they need to learn. He places his hand on the wounded child and the redeemed child in us, silencing the voice which sounds so rational and wants to tell us that there are more important things to do than to deal with the child in us. This is the riot of wasteful wonderment and delight that the Holy Spirit incites in our once dreary lives when we're rescued and set free from bondage to religion and irreligion.

Paul Tillich, an influential thinker of the last century, determined that ignoring or disregarding opportunities to waste ourselves is as destructive as the lack of love that some endure in their early years. Acknowledging the creative nature of God in whose image we are made, he expressed concern about how we ignore the ways religious fundamentalism represses that nature within us and causes it to die. Religious people are sometimes sick, not only because they've been denied love but also because they're not free to love, to waste themselves and their possessions. When they're set free, their inspiring work finds its expression in endless acts of creative service, sometimes uniquely in wood, stone, paint, thread, dance, drama and melody. Free at last, they relish creative life in the heart of God while the religious elite sneer, objecting that these things are pointless, wasteful, impractical and unspiritual.

A Holy Inefficient Life

Not long after Henri Nouwen's death, Philip Yancey wrote a stirring tribute titled "The Holy Inefficiency of Henri Nouwen." Yancey began with his recollection of a meal shared with a group of writers. Richard Foster and Eugene Peterson spoke of an intense young man who'd sought their spiritual counsel and of how they had answered his questions in a letter, recommending books that might be helpful. When someone mentioned that the same inquirer had also contacted Henri Nouwen, Richard Foster remarked, "You won't believe what Nouwen did. He invited this stranger to live with him for a month so he could mentor him in person."

Trained in Holland as a psychologist and theologian, Nouwen spent his early years on an upwardly mobile track in academia, teaching at Notre Dame, Yale and Harvard, writing more than a book a year, and traveling widely as a conference speaker. "He had a résumé to die for," wrote Yancey "which was the problem exactly. The pressing schedule and relentless competition were suffocating his own spiritual life."

After years of searching, Nouwen became priest in residence at Daybreak, a home for the seriously disabled in Toronto. There, Nouwen spent the last ten years of his life, writing, traveling and speaking, but always returning to the refuge of his cherished community.

For several of those years Nouwen assumed responsibility for the care of a young man named Adam. With enormous disabilities—unable to talk, walk or dress himself—Adam offered no sign of comprehension. It took Nouwen nearly two hours to prepare Adam for each day. Bathing and shaving him, brushing his teeth, combing his hair, guiding his hand as he tried to eat—these simple, repetitive acts became for Nouwen like hours of meditation.

"I must admit," wrote Yancey, "I had a fleeting doubt as to whether this was the best use of the busy priest's time. Could not someone else take over the manual chores?" When he cautiously broached the subject with Nouwen, Henri declared that he'd been completely misinterpreted. "I am not giving up anything," he insisted. "It is I, not Adam, who gets the main benefit from our friendship."

I was inspired when I read *Adam: God's Beloved*, Nouwen's personal memoir about his friendship with Adam. Although Adam could not speak and was wracked with violent seizures, Nouwen called Adam "my friend, my teacher, and my guide," and credited Adam with renewing his faith during a particularly dark period of life. Henri acknowledged that physical touch, affection and the messiness of caring for an uncoordinated person were difficult for him. Yet, he had learned to truly love Adam.

In the process he discovered what it must be like for God to love us—"spiritually uncoordinated, retarded, and able to respond with what must seem to God like inarticulate grunts and groans." Through his relationship with Adam, Henri learned the humility and "emptiness" acquired by desert monks after years of determined spiritual discipline.

Before his remarkable life ended, Nouwen concluded that the purpose of our lives is to recognize and acknowledge the face, voice and touch of Jesus in every person we encounter. Because this was the fundamental belief that gave shape to his life, it makes sense that Henri didn't think it was a waste of his time to invite a stranger to live with him for a month, or to dedicate two hours each day to the basic care of Adam. His was a kingdom-of-Jesus-minded economy.

PAUSE TO PONDER

- Take out your calendar and choose when you'll waste an hour or two with God.

- Then decide how you'd like to waste the time: walking through a forest or along a shoreline or simply around the block in the neighborhood where you live. You may prefer instead to gather yourself into a cozy chair with a favorite drink and spend some lingering moments pondering the ways you're choosing to live.

8   Doing What We Can

*"What I do you cannot do; but what you do I cannot do. The needs
are great, and none of us, including me, ever do great things. But we
can all do small things, with great love, and together we can do
something wonderful."*

MOTHER TERESA

It was a gorgeous Labor Day evening. The year was 2007.
Captain Ben Kennedy and I were sitting side by side in rocking
chairs on my brother's back porch. Captain Kennedy was one of
the most significant men to ever enter my life. He was also my
wife's beloved father. While we were enjoying a cold beverage and
grilling burgers, Ben gave me the latest news regarding his declin-
ing health. "Fil, it seems like all I ever do anymore is attend funer-
als and doctor appointments."

There was an awkward silence as he stared off into the distance.
Turning toward me again, he mentioned that he'd been thinking a
lot lately about his mom, who years ago had served as a registered
nurse. "I suspect that if she were still living, Mother wouldn't have
much good to say about modern medicine. I can just about hear
her declaring, 'There comes a time for a person to die, and when
that time comes, it's best to not stand in the way.'"

After another lengthy pause, Ben looked deeply into my eyes
and slowly declared, "Fil, I know that I'm dying."

Caught off-guard by his candor I hastily replied, "Ben, we're all
dying."

Ben Kennedy was one of the kindest and most gentle-spirited men I've ever encountered. During the thirty-five years I knew him, I can't recall him ever speaking a cross word to my wife, my children or me. Nonetheless, in that instant, he gave me a look that seemed to suggest, "Why don't you just keep quiet and let me do the talking." Then he cut a smile, reassuring me he'd thought no such thing.

"Fil, what I mean is that I realize that I'm dying soon, and I wanted you to know that I'm okay with it. I know the Lord loves me, and I recently told him that I'm ready to go whenever that time comes. I truthfully have no fear whenever I think about my life on the other side." Then, with that trademark smile and twinkle in his eyes cherished by all who knew and loved him, he added, "When I told the Lord these things I managed to add, 'If it's just the same with you, I'd sure appreciate it if I didn't have to suffer. And one more thing, Lord, it'd sure be nice if you called me home while I'm sleeping.'"

I'll cherish the memory of those sacred moments till I too am called home. Meanwhile, having gathered my wits, I managed to respond this time with a bit more thoughtfulness than before. "Ben, do you feel okay about asking the Lord for these things?"

"Oh, I suppose so," he slowly replied. "After all, the Lord knows that I trust him, and I know that he loves me."

A few days after our Labor Day visit, it occurred to me that I'd witnessed the ravishing of God's heart. The splendor of a heart that trusts that it's loved gives God more pleasure than all the wonders of the ancient and modern world. Trust is the most cherished gift that we give back to God, and he finds it so captivating that Jesus died for love of it. This, at least in part, explains why the conversation with Ben was so provocative. If there's anything I am certain of regarding Ben's relationship with God it's this: Ben Kennedy unequivocally trusted in Jesus' love for him just as he was.

Our family approached Christmas 2007 aware of the likelihood that this would be "Papa's" last. Sadly and gladly, we were right. On January 6, 2008, after just a few days in the hospital, Captain Ben Kennedy, a retired commercial pilot who often said of himself, "All I ever wanted to do was fly," flew away.

It was an honor to offer my remembrances of Ben at the memorial service attended by hundreds of his family members and friends. Ben lived a full and rich life devoted to those he loved. His unassuming spirit enriched the lives of those who knew and loved him. He was one of the most "at home with himself" people I've ever encountered. He always seemed to be content to live his life doing what he could without worrying too much about what was beyond his ability or control. Ben's authenticity contrasts sharply with those who delude themselves for so long that dishonesty and self-deception become a necessary way of life. *Esse quam videri* reads the coat of arms of early church father Gregory Nazianzen: "To be, rather than appear to be." That is how he will always be remembered, at least by me.

SHE DID WHAT SHE COULD

Like Ben, you and I will someday die. Knowing *when* we will die is beyond our knowledge. Nonetheless, *how* we'll be remembered is within our grasp. Thus we'd be wise to consider how we want to be remembered.

During the past few years I've become gripped by the legacy of the woman who anointed Jesus. Whether consciously or not, the anointing acknowledged Jesus' imminent death and helped him prepare for it. Jesus observed, "She did what she could. She poured perfume on my body beforehand to prepare for my burial" (Mark 14:8 NIV). On the night when she set out for Simon's house with a jar of perfume, we have no way of knowing whether she was aware of the significance of what she was about to do.

More than two thousand years have come and gone since that memorable evening. Ever since she broke her expensive jar of perfume and poured its fragrance on his head, her story has been told. The reason for her immortal legacy is captured in these simple words: "She did what she could."

The significance that Jesus assigns to this story must never be dismissed, ignored or forgotten. Regardless of her intentions or our appraisal of its importance, Jesus received her gift as an act of worship and elevated and honored her for it, declaring that wherever the gospel is preached this beautiful act would also be told in memory of her. All who wish to bring pleasure to God's heart would be wise to take a lesson from her.

Something that I can't help wondering is whether she was aware of the implications of her provocative action. If it was gratitude or affection alone that she wished to convey, she could have expressed those sentiments by washing his feet. Anointing someone's head was a ritual reserved for the conferring of royalty. *Messiah* means "anointed one," yet no one else was declaring that Jesus was the Messiah, at least not openly and without fear of criticism or reprisal. No one had yet anointed him or proclaimed that he was God's promised Messiah! What a prophetic and priestly act she performed by anointing Jesus' head with her expensive perfume!

Regardless of her level of awareness regarding Jesus' divinity, this woman's actions were marked by Jesus as supremely important. But why did Jesus tie her deed with the good news? Why did he guarantee that this anointing will never be forgotten? Jesus unveiled the obvious truth when he declared, "She did what she could!" Yes, that's it. What else could it be? She did *what she could.*

The message of this story is clear: Doing what you are able to do is essential. Jesus wants his followers to do what they can. Yet, I confess that whenever I ponder my legacy, how I hope to be remembered, it's much more grand than *Fil Anderson: He did what he could.*

To be painfully honest, whenever I consider how I'd like my life to be remembered, an avalanche of superlatives floods my imagination: remarkable, amazing, grand, impressive, magnificent, noble, handsome and striking are but a few. Truthfully, any of these words would be appreciated.

Sometimes my deep yearning for love and respect rages wildly out of control. At other times I tend to deflect every kind and affirming word that comes my way. My dismissals and denials are usually more excessive than the praise. Whenever someone says something to me like, "That was an inspiring talk," the only thing I can say is, "You're kind to say that, but you know it was disorganized and way too long." When I'm told by someone that my insights were helpful, I'm quick to say something like, "I'm sure there are others you would have enjoyed hearing speak more than me." Sadly, I do this hoping that it will appear to them to be humility, yet obviously it's not.

Sometimes I'm like the character Garrison Keillor describes in his bestseller *Lake Wobegon Days* who was "starved for a good word, but . . . no word is quite good enough. 'Good' isn't good enough." Beneath the thin veneer of my fraudulent modesty lies a "monster of greed. I drive away faint praise, beating my little chest, waiting to be named Sun-God, King of America, Idol of Millions, Bringer of Fire, The Great Haji, Thun-Dar The Boy Giant." If this makes you laugh, please understand that I'm not trying to be funny; I'm telling the truth. As pathetic as it sounds, sometimes when I'm offered a sincere affirmation, I don't want to say, "Thanks, I'm glad you liked it." I want to say, "Rise to your feet my people. Remove your faces from the carpet, stand and look me in the eyes."

This is part of the reason why my life has sometimes become so dangerously out of control. Lots of days I've been wildly driven to *do* more, *be* more and *have* more. Some days it seems there may not be an end to my craving for more. More money. More things. More friends. More accomplishments. More compliments. More recognition. More respect. More! More! More! What this ultimately means is that no matter what I do, some days I'm simply not content being who I am. Therefore I feel a desperate need to be, to do and to have more than I possibly can. I'm obviously not content to follow the example of the woman who, in Jesus' words, "did what she could."

A Soul Obsession

It's a soul obsession that hounds me every day. Sometimes I recognize it in me and sense it in those around me. Other times I'm oblivious. While striving to earn love and respect from those around us, we search for contentment and the kind of life we dream of some day living. We take our place in the race and watch our lives disappear in the daily grind. We hurry through the present toward some future that's supposed to be better but only turns out to be busier. Meanwhile someone keeps moving the finish line farther away and raising the bar ever higher.

Our jobs have become almost everything to us. We build our lives around them and the benefits they provide. Productivity, success and efficiency drive us. It's no wonder that our days are so often devoid of meaning and our lives a reflection of The Rolling Stones' unforgettable lyric, "I can't get no satisfaction." It's not necessarily the work itself that's killing us, it's the way we give it such meaning and power and control over our lives.

Recently I was the speaker for a weekend family retreat. While engaging in open conversations with moms, dads and their kids, I was struck by the pressure the children feel to not get "lapped" by their peers.

"She's not really good at soccer and she doesn't really like it, but all her friends are doing it," said the mother of a nine-year-old.

"If I miss a practice, even for a doctor's appointment, I get benched," a thirteen-year-old explained.

"If my son didn't have an after-school activity every day of the week, he'd sit around eating junk and playing video games," the father of a ten-year-old confessed.

"I don't really like lacrosse, but I have to do it because it'll look good on my college transcript," a sixteen-year-old confided.

"She wants to take gymnastics, art, dance and tennis. I'm not pushing her. She has to eliminate something!" exclaimed the mother of a seven-year-old.

"I don't have anything scheduled on Sunday afternoons. That's when I have my life," a fourteen-year-old reasoned.

Clearly, some of these kids have too much to do and not enough time in which to do it. But it's difficult to discern whether the parents are pushing or the kids are trying to keep up with their peers. Whatever the cause, one thing's certain—for some kids something's got to give. The problem is apparent: parents and children alike are succumbing to a culture that has lost touch with the meaning of the word *enough*. For this reason, enough is never enough.

WHY ARE WE LIVING THIS WAY?

We live in a frenzied, chaotic world under siege of constant busyness and noise. The weapons of mass distraction and self-destruction are everywhere. We're daily bombarded by millions of advertisements. Many of our lives offer proof that followers of Jesus are not exempt. We're designed to experience full joy, yet many only experience full schedules. We're promised abundant life, yet the experience of many is an abundance of shame, disappointment, fatigue and sadness. Sooner or later we must ask, Why are we living this way?

Based on two highly acclaimed PBS documentaries, *Affluenza: The All-Consuming Epidemic* uses the amusing metaphor of a disease to confront the damage done—to our personal health, our families, our communities and our environment—by the obsessive pursuit of the American Dream.

"Imagine, if you will," the authors write in the introduction, "the following scene."

> In his office, a doctor offers his diagnosis to an attractive, expensively dressed female patient. "There's nothing physically wrong with you," he says. His patient is incredulous. "Then why do I feel so awful?" she asks. "So bloated and sluggish? I've got a big new house, a brand new car, a new wardrobe, and I just got a big raise at work. Why am I so miserable, doctor? Isn't there some pill you can give me?" The doctor shakes his head. "I'm afraid not," he replies. "There's no pill for what's wrong with you." "What is it, doctor?" she asks, alarmed. "Affluenza," he answers gravely. "It's the new epidemic. It's extremely contagious. It can be cured, but not easily."

Meanwhile, evangelical Christians pledge allegiance to biblical standards having to do with money, sex, power, race, the environment, the list goes on; yet most are living just like the rest of the world. Don't you agree that even the most spiritually blind person should be able to see that we as a society are caught up in the modern-day plague of materialism and overconsumption? Can't we see that the epidemic is killing our bodies and our souls? When has a soul ever been satisfied by the temporal things it's prone to strive to attain?

Consider the lives of countless beautiful and famous people. Their names and the tragic stories of their lives routinely flood the media. Far too often their lives offer tragic reminders to us that beauty and fame aren't able to deliver what our hearts yearn for most deeply.

George Eastman's goal in life was financial success. And he reached it. In camera shops throughout the world, products bearing the Eastman Kodak label continue to abound. Yet reaching his goal didn't satisfy his appetite. One morning he spoke with his business associates and then went to his room, where he wrote these words on a piece of paper: "My work is finished. Why wait?" He then put a handgun to his head and ended his life.

Consider the life of Ernest Hemingway. Winner of the Nobel Prize for literature, he was renowned for his overpowering character descriptions in such works as *A Farewell to Arms, For Whom the Bell Tolls* and *The Old Man and the Sea*. Though Hemingway was tremendously talented and accomplished, lack of fulfillment combined with an abundance of misery drove him to take his own life.

In 1923 a prestigious group of overachievers assembled at the Edgewater Beach Hotel in Chicago. Among them were some of the world's most successful financiers: Charles Schwab, president of Bethlehem Steel; Samuel Insull, president of the world's largest utility company; Richard Whitney, president of the New York Stock Exchange; Albert Fall, member of the U.S. president's cabinet; Jesse Livermore, head of the world's largest investment firm; Ivan Kruger, leader of the greatest monopoly in the world; and Leon Fraser, president of the Bank of International Settlement.

This elite gathering is impressive—until we discover the closing chapter of each of their lives. Charles Schwab died bankrupt and lived the last five years of his life on borrowed money. Samuel Insull lived the last days of his life financially destitute as a fugitive in a foreign country. Richard Whitney and Albert Fall were respectively released from federal prison and granted a pardon so they could die at home. Each of the final three mentioned—Livermore, Kruger and Fraser—took his own life.

These tragic stories come as no real surprise to people who have encountered Jesus Christ. Followers of Jesus understand that real purpose and fulfillment in life come through an encounter and ongoing relationship with God.

HARD TO EXPLAIN AND IMPOSSIBLE TO UNDERSTAND

Harder to explain and sometimes impossible to understand is the emptiness, loneliness and disappointment that followers of Jesus sometimes experience. How does a well-intentioned and faithful servant who has accomplished great things for God wind up with a worn-out body housing an empty soul? In this very condition and with these questions on his mind, Mike Yaconelli asked Henri Nouwen for permission to visit him several years ago at his L'Arche Daybreak home in Richmond Hill, Ontario.

On his first morning there he sat in a circle with Henri, other staff members and some of the intellectually challenged of Daybreak. Mike expressed his initial uneasiness with some of the residents who drooled, made grunting sounds, rocked back and forth in their chairs, and slept. When Mike was invited to explain the reason for his visit, he told the group about his hurried and harried life, about how he was trapped on a treadmill of speaking engagements, writing deadlines, management hassles and travel, while also trying to pastor a church and maintain relations with his wife and kids. Finally, he told them he had come to Daybreak because he knew that the treadmill he was on was the same one Henri had escaped. He confessed that he wanted to get away from it all, to withdraw from everyone he knew, to start over. But he painfully admitted that he didn't know how. His life was out of control, and he badly needed help.

During a break, Mike was on his way to the men's room when one of the intellectually challenged residents approached him. Standing uncomfortably close, he suddenly poked Mike in the chest with his finger. "Busy!" the man loudly announced, appearing proud of himself for having discerned Mike's problem.

Mike admitted that instinctively he received the appraisal as a compliment. "Yes, that's right," Mike replied. "That's exactly right. I'm busy." After all, in Mike's world the longer you work and the more exhausted you are, the more status you seem to have. Nobody wants to be in the shameful position of having to admit that they're so insignificant that they don't have too much to do.

While he was still acknowledging how busy he was, the man poked Mike in the chest again, this time even harder, and with his voice louder and firmer declared, "Too busy!" This time Mike felt embarrassed and a bit annoyed. "You got it, pal. That's my problem." But deep inside he wanted this harassing person to simply back off and leave him alone. Until he looked into the man's eyes and saw them filling with tears. The resident began to cry in earnest now, and through his sobs he asked a one-word question that Mike insisted had haunted him ever since: "Why?"

In that watershed moment Mike realized that was the question he had come to Daybreak to answer. Out of the mouth of this innocent, compassionate stranger with intellectual challenges had come wisdom in the form of a simple question.

HOW DOES SUCCESSFUL LIVING APPEAR?

Successful living, according to the counsel of God's written Word, is seeking, knowing, loving and obeying God. Naturally if we seek, we will know; and if we know, we will love; and if we love, we will obey. Meanwhile, "What good would it do to get everything you want and lose you, the real you?" asked Jesus. "What could you ever trade your soul for?" (Mark 8:36-37).

We live in a world that awards love and respect on the basis of possessions, accomplishments and reputations. Within this context our great need is to recognize our incalculable and uncondi-

tional worth to God. I continually encounter people whose drive
to acquire, achieve and be recognized is the cause of their emptiness, disappointment and loneliness.

The problem for many of us is that our days are occupied with
wanting to be somewhere other than where we are, doing things
other than what we've been led to believe must be done, or wishing
we were someone other than who we are. We compare ourselves.
We wish we were as wealthy, popular, gifted, intelligent, spiritual or
attractive as others. These comparisons make us feel ashamed, angry and jealous. It is essential for us to realize that our calling to
follow Jesus is rooted in where we are, the gifts we've been granted
and the challenges that lay before us. Each one of us is unique, a
one-of-a-kind expression of God's unspeakable creativity. We have
a calling that is uniquely ours in the concrete context of the here
and now. It's imperative for us to understand that we will never find
our special place by determining whether we're better or worse than
others. We must learn to trust that we've already been given all that
is needed to be the person God has called us to be in the world.

More than any other threat, comparing ourselves to others robs
us of a good portion of our freedom and contentment. Someone
aptly labeled the tyrant "comparison" as the "thief of joy." When
we're preoccupied with comparing ourselves to others, we ignore
the sage who advised: "Be who you is, 'cause if you ain't who you
is, you is who you ain't." This inevitably leads to the loss of our
freedom, and the next thing we know we're living as prisoners in
the house of fear and sadness. Once we wind up there, we're des-
tined to become shackled by countless fears that fall into one category or another. Either we're afraid of not getting something we
want or losing something we already have. In the end we resemble
Israel Schwartz, who found himself devastated because he wasn't
like Moses. One night an angel appeared to him and said, "On
Judgment Day, Yahweh will not ask you why you were not Moses;

he will ask you why you were not content to be his beloved Izzy."

Truly free people have come to terms with themselves. They know who they are and have embraced their uniqueness. They recognize their gifts and use them with appreciation. They have discovered their place in life and claim it with gladness and humility. Truly free persons are glad for the opportunities they are given each day to do whatever they can.

People who are content to do what they can face the same external pressures as everyone else. They know the distractions of our consumer society, feel job pressures, and care about their obligations to family and friends. Yet they are not enslaved by these external forces. Free persons have a relationship with God that assures them of acceptance; they experience the grace and peace of God as the neutralizer of guilt and shame. And the promise of eternal life, an unrivaled gift from God, frees these children of God from the agonizing fear of death.

Can you imagine experiencing this kind of freedom? Free to be yourself, free in spite of your circumstances, free from your own accusing heart and free from your fear of the future. Free to do no more and no less than what you can do. Isn't this the freedom we yearn for? Because they offer us such tremendous encouragement, let's take a look at some of Jesus' followers who have done whatever they can.

MOTHER TERESA OF CALCUTTA

The awarding of the Nobel Peace Prize to this humble nun in 1979 provoked a massive chorus of disapproval among those who were accustomed to seeing it awarded to political or religious leaders with more visibility and clout. Was Mother Teresa, they persisted with their questions, accomplishing things that made her deserving of the world's most venerable recognition for peacemaking?

I'm so pleased that they didn't consult her for an opinion. When told she had won the Nobel Peace Prize for bringing hope and dignity to millions of unwanted, neglected and uncared-for people, she said: "I am unworthy." Like Francis of Assisi, after whom she modeled her life, she was simply doing what she could by devoting her life wholeheartedly to caring for the poorest of the poor. She was always the first to insist that she was doing nothing special: just washing rotten sores on the withering bodies of the dying, assisting lepers, feeding the starving, providing homes for orphans, and loving the unloved, unwanted, abandoned and forgotten.

Years ago a prominent businessperson who had recently returned from Calcutta after volunteering alongside Mother Teresa and her Sisters of Charity recalled watching Mother Teresa gently bathe the oozing sores of a man so near death that his body had begun to decompose. Turning to his companion he whispered, "I wouldn't do what she's doing for a million dollars!" Overhearing his remark, Mother Teresa turned, looked toward him and with a gentle smile said, "Neither would I!"

Mother Teresa was always modest when explaining her manner of caring:

> I never look at the masses as my responsibility. I look only at the individual. I can love only one person at a time. I can feed only one person at a time.
>
> Just one, one, one.
>
> You get closer to Christ by coming closer to each other. As Jesus said, "Whatever you do to the least of my brethren, you do it to me." So you begin . . . I begin.
>
> I picked up one person—maybe if I didn't pick up that one person I wouldn't have picked up all the others. The whole work is only a drop in the ocean. But if we don't put the drop in, the ocean would be one drop less.
>
> Same thing for you. Same thing in your family. Same thing in the church where you go. Just begin . . . one, one, one.

Although I never met Mother Teresa, her message and methods remind me of my beloved friend John Staggers, an African American and another of God's humble servants. In the heart of Washington, D.C., John did what he could for "the least of these" through a program he envisioned and named Adopt-A-Block. John believed that people fail to do what they can when they become overwhelmed by needs that are greater than they can respond to. On numerous occasions I listened to John challenge churches and individuals to do what they could. "Don't let what you can't do keep you from doing what you can. Don't be overwhelmed by the needs of an entire city. Adopt a block!"

Both John Staggers and Mother Teresa put their finger precisely on the issue that most often prevents us from doing what we can. By focusing on critical concerns in the macrocosm, many people give up before they ever get going. Mother Teresa, John Staggers and countless other unknown saints have done what they could in the microcosm, where they were intimately acquainted with vast needs while trusting God to use their small efforts. These followers of Jesus didn't allow the apparent insignificance of doing what they could to discourage, overwhelm or immobilize them. Instead they persisted in doing what they could for Jesus, whose presence they recognized in the dying and destitute.

Mother Teresa spoke on behalf of an untold number of people who across time have faithfully done what they could when she explained, "I am nothing. He is all. I do nothing on my own. He does it. This is what I am, God's pencil. A tiny bit of pencil with which he writes what he likes."

BILLY GRAHAM

The story about how God chose the humble farm boy Billy Graham from just outside Charlotte, North Carolina, and made him into one of the greatest spiritual leaders of the twentieth century is truly amazing. In the flyleaf of his autobiography, *Just as I Am*, the publisher noted, "Billy Graham Crusades have reached more than 200 million people in person, and millions more have heard him on radio, television, and film. He has been welcomed behind the Iron Curtain, into China and North Korea, and on every continent."

Those who know him best don't typically talk about his accomplishments or the number of people he's stood before to preach. Instead they talk of his unrivaled humility. In 1992 Dr. Graham was interviewed by Diane Sawyer on *Primetime Live*. He was sitting somberly when the last question was posed: "What do you want people to say about you when you're gone?"

His response was immediate and clear. "I don't want people to say anything about me. I want them to talk about my Savior. The only thing I want to hear is Jesus saying, 'Well done, my good and faithful servant.'" Then he bowed his head and said softly and sincerely, "But I'm not sure I'm going to hear that." It appeared to be a rare but honest look into the true nature of Billy Graham's heart. Despite all that he has done for others and the work of God's kingdom, he stills sees himself unworthy of God's approval. In Billy Graham's mind and heart, he has simply done what he could.

When the Disney-style museum opened its doors in his hometown of Charlotte, North Carolina, I followed the news with rapt attention, as did many others around the world. I was fortunate to view a live television broadcast as hundreds of friends, family members, ministers and politicians gathered to dedicate the facility and to celebrate the ministry of Dr. Graham. Former president George H. W. Bush delivered the keynote address. His voice cracked into a sob as he said that Graham was "the man, the preacher, the humble farmer's son who changed the world." Former presidents Jimmy Carter and Bill Clinton also spoke of how Dr. Graham had transformed their lives.

In poor health and rarely appearing in public now, Billy Graham approached the podium using a walker and noted the air of completion and twilight that marked the speeches before his.

"I feel like I've been attending my own funeral, listening to all these speeches," he said as the crowd responded with nervous laughter. "I've been here at the library once, and my one comment when I toured it was that it is too much Billy Graham. My whole life has been to please the Lord and honor Jesus, not to see me and think of me."

LUIS CATALDO

Looking back on my twenty-five-year career with Young Life, one of the highlights was the month-long summer assignments at one of their resort properties. One of those summers I directed a team of high school and college volunteers. These remarkable students had devoted a month of their summer to work without pay at various jobs around the camp. Months prior to their arrival I received numerous letters from many of them expressing their interest in specific jobs. Typically the requests were for the more pleasurable tasks, such as horse wrangling, lifeguarding or mixing milk shakes in the snack bar. However, Luis Cataldo's letter was unlike any other I received. His began with a graphic description of an accident he had survived in which his fingers were badly mangled. He then requested a specific position, assuring me that despite the injury to his hands, he was fully capable of doing an excellent job.

"Mr. Anderson, would you prayerfully consider my request to serve on the 'pit crew'? I'd especially like to be at the first station." Luis was asking me to let him be the person who scraped the leftover food from the bowls and plates of the four hundred guests who had eaten at every meal.

Rereading his letter with baffled curiosity, I wondered what his motives were. Rather than ask questions, I chose to grant his wish. My initial impressions of Luis were strongly positive; he was determined to serve others and seemed to have a keen awareness of Jesus' love and acceptance. Nonetheless, as I stood in the shadows of the steamy, hot kitchen in the middle of the summer watching him scrape food from bowls and plates and place them in racks, I remained curious about his motive.

Finally, a couple of weeks into the month I asked him if he would answer a question I had. Before I could pose my question, for what felt like the umpteenth time he said, "Fil, thank you so much for giving me the job I requested. It's turned out to be precisely what I hoped it would be."

"Luis, that's the question I wanted to ask you," I said. "Why did you request this job? What were you hoping for?"

"Well," he replied, "You see, several months ago I began talking with God about my desire to do everything I could to serve every person coming to camp. One day it occurred to me that if I had this job, three times a day, every day for a month, I could pray for each person as I scrape their plate." I sat in stunned amazement. What a servant's heart! He ended our visit saying, "I love doing what I can."

Those simple words, so similar to the words Jesus used to describe the woman who anointed him with perfume, herald the one thing that all of God's greatest servants share in common: They did what they could.

LYNDA JADICK HARRIS

Lodged in our heart is the power to give others the courage to do what they can. Isn't that amazing? Our affirmation of others is very powerful.

Lynda recognized that power, and it pleased her to observe its effect, especially in her daughters' lives. At the service of celebration for Lynda's life, her daughter Juli recalled, "From day one,

Mom has been the constant force of encouragement and love in my life. Each day before Carrie [Lynda's younger daughter] and I went to school, Mom would say, 'Have a grand and glorious day, because Jesus Christ lives big in you.' Then she'd remind us of Philippians 4:13, 'You can do all things through Christ who strengthens you.'"

That simple daily routine has proven more powerful than Lynda ever imagined. I'm confident that she thought she was doing "what she could," and that's the beauty of it. Thus as her life was being remembered, the touch of her affirmation compelled Juli to do what she could by affirming, "Mom loved everyone unconditionally. Mom touched people in a way that so few do. When you were with her you felt special and loved."

Finally, Juli declared, "Carrie and I feel very scared and lonely based on the fact that both of our parents have passed away. We really need this supportive network of friends Mom built to be our surrogate parents. And Mom, I'd like to say, 'Thank you for doing what you could to love us, care for us, to make us laugh, and for rooting us on into the love of Jesus.'"

Those simple words, so similar to the words Jesus used to describe the woman who anointed him, herald the one thing that all of God's greatest servants share in common: They did what they could.

WHAT IF?

I can't help wondering, *What if I lived my life that way? What if we all decided to do what we could?* The possibilities blow my mind! Just think how much more of God's will would be done and how much more of God's kingdom would come on earth if we decided to spend all of our time and energy, as Jesus did, emptying ourselves of our own self-serving agendas and devoting ourselves to doing what we can.

I've got to be honest: The thought both excites and terrifies me. It causes me to wonder just how different I could stand for my life to be.

A dear friend once told me that when he considers his life and the other followers of Jesus in his little corner of the world, he can't help picturing someone dressed in one of those deep sea diving suits. You know the kind—the one worn in *Twenty Thousand Leagues Under the Sea*. The huge bell-shaped helmet, a thick canvas suit covering the body and heavy steel-toe boots. And there they are, standing in a bathtub in two inches of water, wondering, *What am I doing here wearing all of this equipment?* Then my friend explained how self-consumed and safe his religion had trained him to become. How woefully less than what he imagined God had intended.

Our son Lee, with a fire in his belly to care for orphans in Africa, sat down last winter with the youth pastor of our church and searched through a catalog of World Vision relief projects. Together they were hoping to identify a project the youth group could rally around. Knowing that water is life in drought-ravaged African villages, they kept coming back to a well-drilling project that would provide safe water to a Zambian village. The only reason they hesitated was the price tag: $12,500.

Ours is a midsize inner-city church. The youth group consists of lower- and middle-class adolescents. Despite the odds, they decided to pray about the idea. A week later they agreed, "What the heck? That's more money than we could hope to get our hands on. What is there to lose? Since we know that only God could make this happen, let's simply do what we can."

During the next four months the youth group members did what they could, putting together a wild variety of events and projects. There were concerts, bake sales, basketball tournaments and a video game competition. And they prayed. Doing what they could never became a burden.

Finally, on a Sunday morning in mid-May, Lee stood before the youth group and asked everyone to listen carefully. With disappointment written across his face and apparent sadness causing his voice to crack, he announced (as other members of the youth group rushed in spraying everyone with Super Soaker water guns), "It's a miracle! We did what we could, and the Zambian village is getting a well!"

Pause to Ponder

- Looking back on your life, what do you see? Does it reflect the values and investments you wish to be remembered for? Has it been a waste or a beautiful thing to Jesus?

- Looking ahead, what are your hopes for the future when your life here ends? What will your legacy be? Would you like to hear Jesus say that your life was a beautiful thing for the simple reason that you did what you could? The decision is yours.

9 The Gift of Memory

"I meant to accomplish a good bit today. Instead I keep thinking: Will the next generation of people remember to drain the pipes in the fall? I will leave them a note."

ANNIE DILLARD

To simply remember may be the most important thing you ever remember to do.

Remembering was high on Moses' to-do list. Thus, in no uncertain terms, he declared "take care and watch yourselves closely, so as neither to forget the things that your eyes have seen nor to let them slip from your mind all the days of your life; make them known to your children and your children's children" (Deuteronomy 4:9 NRSV).

"Memory believes before knowing remembers," writes William Faulkner in his brilliant novel *Light in August*. The brilliant and effectual force of our memories must never be ignored, denied or taken for granted. In everyone's life there are experiences so rich and profound that even before our minds can consciously process all the reasons for our reactions and emotions, our memories are interacting with our present realities to inform us viscerally and instinctively how we should feel and react in a certain moment.

AN ABSOLUTE NECESSITY
We'll never fully enjoy our life until we realize that our capacity to

remember is an astounding gift and its utilization an absolute necessity. For most of us this poses a problem, since our memory is something we probably rarely think about until we get to the age where we have trouble remembering. Then suddenly we're spending a lot of time looking for our car keys and reading glasses. We're scrambling family names and calling our sons by the names of our brothers, our granddaughters by the names of our daughters. We're forgetting the names of people we met last week. We're forgetting what we did last week.

It's no wonder that one of the most dreaded maladies confronting individuals and families today is a disease known as Alzheimer's. The heinous sickness viciously destroys brain cells, obliterating memory and erasing the victim's history. Cherished memories of holidays, vacations and birthday celebrations are forgotten. All the laughter, all the tears, all the joys and heartaches, all the love that was shared, the words that were spoken, all that was given and received slowly fades. Those stricken by this illness lose a bit more of their motor skills and of their minds every day. At last there's nothing left to lose except life itself.

Facing the dreadful prospect of losing our memory may help us see how precious our ability to remember truly is. Without our memory we'd be unable to take pleasure in the good things that have happened to us and for us. Fond memories encourage us, lift us when we're feeling down and help sustain the hope we've been given to treasure in our hearts. It's no wonder that when people are asked what items they'd retrieve if their homes were about to be destroyed, they typically refer to things associated with the preservation of memories, such as photographs, videos and journals.

Our memory is one of the largest contributors to our identity and sense of being. Our sorrows and joys, our feelings of anguish and contentment, do not merely rely on the events of our lives, but also, maybe even more so, on the ways we remember them. Perhaps the events are less significant than the place we assign them in our lives, and the way they shape and define us within the context of our life's story. For instance, different people remember a similar sickness, misfortune, accomplishment or surprise in very different ways. Much of their sense of self comes less from what happened than from how they remember what happened, how they have placed the past events into their own personal story.

It's not surprising, then, that most of our emotions are closely tied to our memory. Sorrow is a bitter memory, shame is an accusing memory, gratitude is a pleasant memory, and all such emotions are profoundly influenced by the way we've incorporated our memory of past events into our way of being in the world. We actually perceive and experience the world with our memories. Our memories help us to observe and process new experiences and give them a place in our vastly unique life experiences.

Truly one of the most consequential forces in the shaping of our life is our capacity to remember. Yet equally significant is our ability to choose to forget. A memory recalled or ignored, denied or forgotten may prove momentous. A single memory may possess enough force to make any one of us feel immense shame, sadness, anger or gladness. Therefore, the most vital challenge for a follower of Jesus often is to simply remember.

God Constantly Urges Us to Remember

Is it any wonder then that God constantly urges us to remember? From the Bible's opening words, telling us how the world appeared, right up to its closing words, telling us how creation will one day become new, much of what the Bible insists on can be summed up in a simple word: *Remember.* Throughout its pages, a swarm of prophets, poets, preachers and Jesus constantly assure us that just as God faithfully remembers all things, we too must be consumed with remembering.

The Bible leaves no room for doubt: of all the important things for us to remember, none rivals our need to remember God. Both the Old and New Testaments echo the clarion call to remember God's presence always with us, reflected brilliantly in his unsurpassed power and unrelenting affectionate nature. From its beginning to the end, the Bible stresses the importance of remembering God's flawless character and exquisite plan for creation.

God left nothing to chance when he inspired Isaiah to record this autobiographical depiction of his unrivaled persona.

I'm first, I'm last, and everything in between.
I'm the only God there is.
Who compares with me? . . .
Have you ever come across a God, a real God, other than me?
There's no Rock like me that I know of. . . .

Remember these things. . . .
Take it seriously . . . that you're my servant.
I made you, *shaped* you. . . .
I'll never forget you. (Isaiah 44:6-8, 21, italics for *remember* added)

Life would be so much simpler, richer and more complete if only we'd remember what God says and does. However, understanding that our greater need is for reminders than for instructions, God graciously reveals that even he isn't willing to risk forgetting. Therefore, promising Noah that a flood would never again destroy the earth, God reassured him, "I have set my rainbow in the clouds, and it will be the sign of the covenant between me and the earth. . . . Whenever the rainbow appears in the clouds, I will see it and *remember*" (Genesis 9:13, 16 NIV, italics added). We must learn from God to become seers like God; we must remember.

Most every day for the past several years I've offered a prayer for Lucie and our family that I recorded in the back of my Bible. It reflects my particular desire for them to see and thus remember God. Most of the words I borrowed from one of the apostle Paul's prayers (see Ephesians 1:17-20):

> Abba of Jesus please make those whom I love wise and discerning in their knowledge of You. May the eyes of their heart be focused and clear so that they can know and understand the extraordinary plan you have for them . . . and what is the immeasurable and unlimited and surpassing greatness of your power in and for them and all who believe, as demonstrated in the working of your mighty strength, which you exerted in Christ when you raised him from the dead and seated him at your right hand in heaven.

Forgetting and dismantling the impoverished, traditionalist, legalistic and fictitious perceptions of God that religion imparts are as essential as remembering the truth regarding God. For instance, I've had to dismiss the notion of an angry god disgusted with my immaturity, the cranky god whose moods change with my behavior, the prejudiced god whose mean-spirited values match mine, the weak and needy god who relies on me for assistance, the doctrinaire god whose theology strictly adheres to mine, the hawkish god who sanctions my "right" to kick the butt of anyone who threatens or endangers me, the fickle god who loves me conditionally, and the plethora of other gods who have held me captive in the house of fear. The list seems endless.

God's invitation into intimate union runs counter to the dogmatic ranting of certain religious leaders, proponents of legalistic morality and rigid rule keepers. The scandalous love of the invisible God is made clearly visible in Jesus Christ who says, "Live in me. Make your home in me just as I do in you" (John 15:4). When

Jesus talks about "home," he means a place of indescribable intimacy; it's a place of tender warmth and hospitable love, of safety, gracious acceptance and endless expressions of affection.

God longs for us to remember that our identity is summed up in this simple affirmation: "I belong to my lover, / and his desire is for me" (Song of Songs 7:10 NIV). The kingdom of God happens whenever we experience the wild, raging assurance that we're unequivocally God's beloved. Yet some of us will first need to forget what our religious training taught us: that God's acceptance and affection is reserved for "I think I can, I think I can" strivers after God, driven by guilt and fixated on "graceless getting worthy" by sheer grit and determination.

Until the unlimited, unbridled and unrelenting love of God takes root in our life, until God's reckless pursuit of us captures our imagination, until our head knowledge of God settles into our heart through pure grace, nothing really changes. Idolatrous devotion to religion makes us arrogant, narrow-minded, elitist and intolerant of any idea that doesn't jive with our religious framework. Thus we must remember that the gospel is for everyone. "It is not reserved for those who are well-known mystics or for those who do wonderful things for the poor," writes Jean Vanier. "[It is for] those poor enough to welcome Jesus. It is for people living ordinary lives and who feel lonely. It is for all those who are old, hospitalized or out of work, who open their hearts in trust to Jesus and cry out for his healing love."

God's Promise Extends to Us

Appearances to the contrary notwithstanding, God's promise to his people living in exile centuries ago extends to us: "I know what I'm doing. I have it all planned out—plans to take care of you, not abandon you, plans to give you the future you hope for" (Jeremiah 29:11). Yet remembering God's promises is difficult when the cheese is sliding off our cracker because life's not unfolding according to our plan. Therefore, at precisely the right moment God reminds us that he's in control. His strategic reminders reflect a love in his heart that's without boundaries, limits or breaking points, and there's no telling how many reminders he has set in place.

When our children were quite young, I recall an Easter Sunday when I hid more Easter eggs than I could imagine them finding. When the hunt began I was alarmed by how slowly they searched. When I asked why, Will explained, "Because I don't want it to ever end."

In similar fashion God has hidden within and around our lives a vast and staggering array of reminders that his promises are true. God's hidden reminders are endless, everywhere and forever. The earth provides a dizzying number of reminders of God's power and attention to detail. Botanists estimate that there are over 240,000 species of flowering plants in the world. God designed and created each plant and star, giving to each a name he remembers. Yet here are too many stars for scientists to actually count one by one. So using other methods they estimate that there are in the neighborhood of 1,000,000,000,000,000,000,000 stars in our universe.

To me, impressive details about God's power, creativity and capacity to remember are meaningful as long as everything's going well. However, when my life or the life of someone I love is headed for hell in a hand basket, or when someone I love is diagnosed with a brain tumor, or when my son's teammate is killed in a head-on car crash, or when a nearly starved Haitian mom begs me to bring her child home with me to America, I could care less about plants and stars. When it's midnight and I'm exhausted and sitting alone in a hotel lounge drinking a beer and feeling lonely, I despise myself for being a fraud because only a few hours earlier I was urg-

ing a crowd to remember the indisputable truth that I've now
clearly forgotten:

> Yahweh your God is in your midst,
> a victorious warrior.
> He will exult with joy over you,
> he will renew you by his love;
> he will dance with shouts of joy for you
> as on a day of festival.
> (Zephaniah 3:17 JB)

These are the times when I need the wild, unrestricted love of
God to blow away with hurricane force the dark clouds of my fear
and dread, bringing instead calm and steady assurance of God's
tenderness and compassion. I need God to hear my anguished
questions or my angry rants, or to sit quietly with me in silence.
Knowing that Jesus experienced the pitch and yaw of despair and
moral struggle, I need him standing beside me when I'm unstable.
In other words I'm downright needy. And because of his character
God provides us endless reminders: In his always-nearer-to-us-
than-our-next-breath presence, in our family and friends, in sun-
rises and sunsets, in smiles and laughter, in songs and silence, in
breezes and stillness, in joy and even in tears, God calls us to remember. And if we'd remember, we would experience the most
full, brave and beautiful life imaginable. However, we keep forgetting the most important thing: *remember God!* And I can't stop
wondering why.

OUR FAILURE OR REFUSAL TO REMEMBER GOD

Our failure or refusal to remember God is the most central cause of
our pain and sadness. When we willfully choose to live on our
own, we can't avoid enslavement to cruel taskmasters posing as
givers of life. Why else would God remind our ancient ancestors in

their forgetful state to "*remember* that you were slaves . . . and that the LORD your God brought you out of there with a mighty hand and an outstretched arm" (Deuteronomy 5:15 NIV, italics added)?

Caught up in an endless and deadly cycle of needing constant reminders, Israel is given a path to follow. God's intent is for the law to serve people (never vice versa) by keeping us anchored in the safe harbor of a God-centered life. God chose Moses to deliver the news. For the umpteenth time God began with the all-important reminder, "I am God, your God, who brought you out of the land of Egypt, out of a life of slavery" (Exodus 20:1-3). In other words, don't forget my unrivaled character because it prohibits me from doing anything that is not good. Then God proceeded to lay down the law. There's not a single negotiable term. God insists that each is essential because each is for our good.

> *Remember:* "No other gods, only me."
>
> *Remember:* "No carved gods."
>
> *Remember:* "No using the name of GOD . . . in curses or silly banter."
>
> *Remember:* "Observe the Sabbath day, to keep it holy."
>
> *Remember:* "Honor your father and mother."
>
> *Remember:* "No murder."
>
> *Remember:* "No adultery."
>
> *Remember:* "No stealing."
>
> *Remember:* "No lies about your neighbor."
>
> *Remember:* "No lusting after your neighbor's house—or wife or servant or maid or ox or donkey."
>
> (See Exodus 20:1-17.)

God marked the milestone moment in breathtaking fashion. It must have been a sight to behold, highlighted by thunder and lightning, a trumpet blast and a smoking mountain. Meanwhile, if the people in attendance had remembered God's character they

would have remembered that they didn't need to be afraid. But
forgetting, they were scared out of their minds and "they pulled
back and stood at a distance. They said to Moses, 'You speak to us
and we'll listen, but don't have God speak to us or we'll die'" (Exodus 20:18-19).

Moses must have understood. Like them, he'd endured cata-
strophic lapses of memory and lost sight of the truth pertaining to
God. Scared to death of God, he'd imagined that God is crazy. But
this time remembering God, Moses compassionately urged the
people: "Don't be afraid. God has come to test you and instill a
deep and reverent awe within you so that you won't sin." However,
"the people kept their distance while Moses approached the thick
cloud where God was" (Exodus 20:20-21).

In similar fashion, remembering God enabled Nehemiah to respond effectively to God's strategic plan. Executing careful analy-
sis, thoughtful planning and teamwork, Nehemiah successfully
fulfilled his mission. Yet, despite his achievement, Nehemiah
faced scorn, slander and threats, as well as fear, conflict and dis-
couragement. By his own account, "They refused to listen and
failed to *remember* the miracles you performed among them. They
became stiff-necked and in their rebellion appointed a leader in
order to return to their slavery." Nonetheless Nehemiah remained
steadfast and true and declared God's unrelenting faithfulness:
"But you are a forgiving God, gracious and compassionate, slow to
anger and abounding in love. Therefore you did not desert them"
(Nehemiah 9:17 NIV).

In Genesis, God is presented as speaking creation into existence.
God simply speaks the word and suddenly it happens: everything
seen and unseen is called into being by God's spoken word.

Seemingly in deliberate parallel to the opening words of Genesis,
the apostle John begins his Gospel account by presenting God as
speaking salvation into existence. Jesus simply speaks the word and

it happens: forgiveness and judgment, mercy and grace, joy and love, death and resurrection. No wonder John noted, "We saw the glory with our own eyes / . . . like Father, like Son" (John 1:14)

Thus whenever God speaks a word, there is unleashed a stunningly creative and life-altering force of limitless power. Each word possesses infinite value. How then could we attempt to defend our failure or refusal to remember each one? Nonetheless stories reflecting our chronic failure to remember God's words appear endless, and the consequence is always the same: "we sat and wept / when we *remembered*" (Psalm 137:1 NIV, italics added). This is everyone's story.

In the four Gospel accounts alone, there appear to be approximately twenty-two occasions when the word *remember* is used. Yet in my opinion the most provocative moment occurs in Simon the Leper's home after the woman anoints Jesus' head with her expensive perfume, setting off a firestorm of controversy. Demanding her critics to back off, Jesus declares, "Wherever the gospel is preached throughout the world, what she has done will also be told, in *memory* of her" (Mark 14:9 NIV, italics added). Fascinating! On the strength of his word, Jesus says that wherever his story is remembered her story will be remembered too.

God's Chief Purpose

Have you ever wondered what God's chief purpose is in giving us memory? Plenty would agree that it has something to do with enabling us to learn from the past. If we didn't get something right the first time, we can have another go at it later. Those holding this notion would likely agree that it's not possible to undo past mistakes or their consequences. Neither would they suggest that we can erase old wounds. However, because of the powerful gift of our memory, we can think, feel and see our way back through our past. In addition, because of the infinite reservoir of power, grace and kindness that Jesus makes available to us, the devastation created by our brokenness can finally be healed.

The horrible things that occurred in our past will always remain a part of who we are. If we choose to ignore or deny them, our broken past will persist in wearing us out, tearing us up, knocking us down or keeping us stuck. Even so, fear of bringing secret wounds into the open drives many people to falsely believe that if they don't think about them, they somehow go away. The problem is: they don't. Unhealed wounds that are hidden set us up for added sin and sorrow in our relations with God and others. This behavior often becomes habitual and is passed on to future generations.

Another possible consequence when we ignore the truth about our past is ending up like Miss Havisham in Charles Dickens's novel *Great Expectations*. The engaged Miss Havisham received a letter on her wedding day at 8:40 a.m. indicating that her husband-to-be was not coming. Rather than ignoring or denying this crushing blow, she stopped all clocks in the house at the exact time the letter arrived and spent the remainder of her life in her bridal dress, wearing only one shoe (since she had not yet put on the other at the time of the tragedy). Even as an elderly lady, she remained crushed by the weight of that devastating blow. It was as if "everything in the room and house had stopped." Rather than ignore or deny it, she chose instead to remain stuck in the past.

Recognizing our memory as God's gift to us, those things we erroneously believe will always be a burden can be redeemed. Absolutely nothing in our lives remains outside the reach of God's redemptive love and mercy. Yet whenever we attempt to hide or deny parts of our life story from God, others and ourselves, we're dangerously assuming a divine role. Thus we become an inappropriate judge of the past and subjugate God's grace and mercy to our own judgment and condemnation. Most tragically, we disconnect from our self- and others-imposed wounds, and from God's wounds suffered *for us*. In the end, if we allow it, our memory enables us to bless the past and be blessed by it, even those dark and painful parts that we used to curse.

Remembering this fundamental principle is always essential: Intimate union with Jesus must include honest reflection on the positive and negative effects of all of our life's encounters. Our family of origin as well as all other major influences in our life must be considered. This hard work is not for the faint of heart. But the extent to which we can go back and understand how it has shaped us will determine, to a large degree, our level of awareness and our ability to break destructive patterns, pass on beneficial legacies, and grow in our relationships with God and other people.

Since the handling of our memories is so delicate, and since the consequences following our discernment about what to do with them goes so far in ultimately determining the quality of all our relations, let's take a closer and more thoughtful look at the matter.

THE STATE OF DENIAL

A few years ago a friend informed me with a suggestive grin that the fastest growing state in America is "the State of Denial." My response was immediate and unedited: "I've maintained a residence there for as long as I can remember." For all I know, Mark Twain was referring to me when he declared, "All men are liars, partial or hiders of facts, half tellers of truths, shirks, moral sneaks."

Everyone knows how to hide and how to pretend. At some point in childhood we all make the amazing discovery that we can manipulate the truth about ourselves. Dating back to Adam and Eve, it often begins with a simple yet not "innocent" lie—frequently a denial of having done something wrong. A more gripping realization is that our capacity for hiding isn't confined to what we say or don't say. Thus we learn to pretend, sometimes referred to as "playing games," and to perfect the art of "packaging and marketing" ourself to others.

Most of us become masters in the art of pretending. (How do I know? It's simple. It takes a pretender to recognize one.) We learn how to appear brave when we feel afraid, how to appear happy when we feel sad, how to appear certain when we feel confused. We also learn to mask hatred with apparent love, anger with apparent peace and apathy with apparent compassion. In a nutshell, we learn how to "pretend," how to present ourself in the necessary light, a light intended to project a positive impression and maintain the appearance of our self-esteem.

Although this charade might appear normal and benign, there is a dark side to hiding and pretending; what starts out as a role, with time and practice, becomes an identity. At first the masks we create reflect how we want others to see us. Over time, however, our masks reflect how we want to see ourself. Eventually we've completely confused the mask with who we are. Our masks have become our identity, and we've become our deceptions and lies. In the process we lose our true self and wind up with a false self that's based on an illusion. On our best days our life's like a hall of smoke and mirrors. On our worst days it's like a house of horrors.

There are few things more difficult to distinguish and dismantle than our most practical and prized illusions. And none of our illusions are harder to identify than those at the core of our false self. The false self is our comfort zone; it's where we imagine being in control. Eventually we become so accustomed to it that we're no longer aware of it. We're so convincing and believable that we become convinced, and we believe it's who we really are.

THE DILEMMA OUR FALSE SELF CREATES

The Russian novelist Leo Tolstoy wrote a short story, *Father Sergius,* that illustrates the dilemma our false self creates. Sergius was a young Russian prince who, heartbroken after a failed romance, abandoned a successful military career to enter the priesthood.

As a priest, Sergius exercised the same discipline that'd made him an ideal soldier. Mastering every requirement of the church, following carefully the orders of his superiors and through strict personal discipline he gained total control over his actions and most of his thoughts. Life for Sergius became a determined pursuit of virtue and holiness.

After several years Father Sergius, having achieved all he thought possible as a parish priest, became disillusioned by the worldliness and arrogance of his peers. So he withdrew and began living as a hermit and soon became renowned for his devotion to prayer, meditation and poverty.

To the simple peasants in the nearby village he became a fascinating mystery. As Sergius's reputation increased, people, and particularly the sick, increasingly began to visit him, seeking his prayers. When he finally agreed to pray for a sick child, miraculously the child became well. The healing resulted in increasing demands on Sergius to minister to the sick and others in despair.

Sergius was provoked by the demands and began to resent the interruptions. He didn't want to be bothered with caring for others. What Sergius wanted most was to be left alone so he could concentrate on righteousness.

It was in this frame of mind that he fell from grace. While ministering to a demanding crowd, he became ill. When a stranger came to his defense and demanded the crowd to leave, Sergius expressed his gratitude by agreeing to pray for the man's manic daughter. Sadly, the most difficult cancer that had persistently and privately plagued Sergius's will was sexual lust. Sergius had wrestled for years with fantasies and now, in a weakened state, and alone with this young lady, he allowed her flirtations to entice and then seduce him. (I wonder how many people there are who, like me, oftentimes battle lust and countless other afflictions all alone.)

Sergius immediately recognized the terrible nature of his immorality. His whole life was shattered as he viewed the devastation of his years of virtue. He desperately sought God in his heart, but it seemed God was not there. He sought God by the banks of a river, but again it seemed God was not there. He sought God in the fields, but God was apparently not there. He prayed, but he felt that his prayers were not heard, and certainly they were not answered.

Sergius fled from his cloistered past, cutting his ties completely. He wandered about, living as a lost and hopeless beggar. He was consumed with anguish, and he lived in utter despair. He no longer had a God to comfort and accompany him. The hope of a perfect life had been shattered forever.

Then, in a dream Sergius was directed by an angel to visit a cousin, a very plain and simple-minded lady. In her, Sergius discovered a woman torn by the conflicting demands of her home, family and community. Though she didn't seem to be religious, she was ready always to share herself and any of her meager possessions with others in need. Sergius began to recognize and be instructed by how his cousin served God through her attention to the needs of others, while he'd tried to gain praise through his devotion to religion.

As Sergius started a new life of compassionate sharing, he gradually felt God begin to reveal himself. Over time the old priest's new faith became forged in the reality that we all sin and fall short of God's glory, and that in the end we all are saved by grace alone, not in the least by our own righteous efforts.

So, what then is the point of Tolstoy's story?

Sergius suffered from unadulterated self-righteous pride. In his case pride played its cunning role perfectly, using even righteousness to destroy a priest's life. Only tragedy, a complete moral failure, brought the humility that Sergius needed to find the true way to God and to his true self. Suffering of some sort seems to be the only thing strong enough to destabilize our arrogance and ignorance. Pride isn't complicated. Pride is simply thinking more highly of ourselves than we have any right to think. Pride is essentially putting me above God. When I fail to remember God, I surmise that I alone control who I am and what I've accomplished. Outrageously I relegate the omnipotent God to second place. This is pride, the gravest of all my sins and the most painful to acknowledge.

Pride's most devastating effect is our failure to remember the most fundamental truth of our existence, that we are not our own but have been bought with a price. One of life's most essential questions is, *When you truthfully consider your life, how much did God give to you and what did you add on our own?*

There's only one true answer. God has given us everything. God gave us our talent, our appearance, our opportunities. God gave us our family and our friends. At times we may have worked hard. But immediately we must remember that God gave us our aspiration, our motivation, our determination and desire. Instead of congratulating ourself for what we've accomplished, we must remember to give God thanks for what God's done for us and remember to be grateful always for the opportunities only God is able to make possible.

GOING BACK TO GO FORWARD

If you've ever been behind the wheel of a car stuck in mud or snow, then it's likely you learned a vitally important lesson that's well worth remembering: *sometimes we have to go back in order to go forward.* People who beam brightly the light of Jesus have gazed deeply into the darkness of their own broken existence. This reality is both very telling and very important to tell. It's telling in the sense that it reveals the central paradox of our predicament: what we yearn for most is also what we fear most—to be known as we truly are.

There are simple reasons for remembering to tell the truth of who we are, even if only to ourselves. Otherwise, we run the terrible risk of losing touch with our true selves and thus adopting the carefully edited version we project in our desperate drive for acceptance.

Susan Howatch's novel *Glittering Images* traces the spiritual journey of Charles Ashworth, an ordained priest in the Church of England. A widower in his late thirties, Charles is devoted to the church and is upright, respected and well-loved by his superiors. He is also a friend of the Archbishop of Canterbury, who asks that he visit a parish to investigate a possibility of moral failure or scandal in another bishop's life.

The disturbing complexity and the stress associated with the situation he encounters pushes Charles over the edge, and he winds up terribly drunk at the front door of a brilliantly discerning spiritual director named Father Darrow who graciously takes Charles into his care.

During his visits with Father Darrow, Charles slowly begins to peel back the layers beneath the surface of the public person he presents to other people, the "glittering image" that is always proper and polished. He begins to realize and acknowledge the negative feelings he's denied and the inconsistencies in his behavior with people. For instance, during his investigative visit he attempted to kiss the bishop's attractive assistant within twenty-four hours of meeting her. He lies in the name of God to accomplish God's work. He secretly drinks too much to numb his pain.

When he's asked by Darrow to be ruthlessly honest and to peel back more of his mask, he makes clear that he can't. Others, such as his father, have "got a colossal hold over me," he explains.

"Who's 'me'?" says Darrow.

"My true self . . . the glittering image."

"Ah yes," says Darrow, "and of course that's the only Charles Ashworth that the world's allowed to see, but you're out of the world now, aren't you, and I'm different from everyone else because I know there are two of you. I'm becoming interested in this other self of yours, the self nobody meets. I'd like to help him come out from behind the glittering image and set down this appalling burden which has been tormenting him for so long."

"He can't come out."

"Why not?"

"You wouldn't like him or approve of him."

Illuminating God's redemptive movement in his life, Charles Ashworth finally acknowledges and meets head-on the stranglehold the glittering image has on his life. He begins to realize the massive amount of time and energy he's devoted to win everyone's recognition and approval. With the prayerful and wise assistance of a spiritual counselor, he begins to uncover why and how he created the false person who'd been living in a "glittering image."

DANGEROUSLY INDEPENDENT FORCES

When we refuse to remember our painful memories, they become dangerously independent forces that can produce a crippling and even deadly effect on our ability to function within God's design. The natural consequence is that we become strangers to ourselves. We edit our history down to a manageable size and adopt the falsehood as our actual life story. Forgetting our past is a criminal act of personal treason. It's like turning our most needed and reliable teacher against us. By refusing to face our painful memories we dismiss an opportunity to have our hearts healed in order for our trust in God to mature. When Jesus said, "Those who are well have no need of a physician, but those who are sick" (Mark 2:17 NRSV), he was affirming that only those willing to face their broken and wounded condition are in a position to be healed and enter into a new way of living.

There is no forgiveness or healing that comes as a consequence of forgetting our wounds. Forgiveness based on forgetfulness is a Christian version of a frontal lobotomy, according to psychologist and writer Dan Allender. Intimate union with Jesus doesn't erase our past. God doesn't give us memory loss or perform plastic surgery on the wounds of our past. God does forgive our past, but he doesn't delete it. When we're adopted into God's family, we have cuts and bruises, broken bones, battle-fatigue syndrome and limbs that were injured in life's war. God's intention is to reset our brokenness and patch up our wounds. Yet he purposely allows our scars and weakness and limps to remain, which I view as God's severe mercy.

In 1944 a horrible atrocity occurred in Sighet, a small town in northern Romania. All of the Jews in the Romanian town were assembled and deported to concentration camps. Elie Wiesel, the novelist who in 1986 was awarded the Nobel Peace Prize, was among them. Surviving the Holocaust, he returned again twenty years later to his home town. What grieved him most was that the people now living in Sighet had erased the Jews from their memory. He explained, "I was not angry with the people of Sighet . . . for having driven out their neighbors of yesterday, nor for having denied them. If I was angry at all it was for having forgotten them. So quickly, so completely . . . Jews have been driven not only out of town but out of time as well." Having survived, Wiesel felt that he owed something to the dead, and that anyone who was guilty of forgetting them was also betraying them again.

Elie Wiesel's story offers us invaluable insight: to forget our sins may be an even greater offense than to commit them. What is forgotten cannot be healed, and whatever remains unhealed enhances the potential for greater evil. By forgetting our past we paralyze our future; forgetting the sin behind us, we evoke the sin before us. Our failure to remember previous failures and mistakes may guarantee that we will repeat them again.

Therefore we should not be surprised whenever our failure to remember leads to our undoing. The power of a single memory to shape our life is immense. Our memories—the good, the bad, the ugly and all the others combined—play a major role in our sense of being. Our joys and sorrows, our feelings of loss and gain, rely not only on the events that have occurred in our lives but even more so on the ways we remember those events. For instance, one of the most fascinating things I've observed in my marriage is how my wife and I remember the same incidents in different ways. Countless times we've remembered the same happy surprise, accomplishment, disappointment or illness in different ways. Looking back on those events indicated that our sense of self had more to do with how we processed what happened than what actually occurred. Hence the Holy Spirit's guidance is imperative in our discernment.

JESUS, REMEMBER ME

"Jesus, remember me." These words express the dying wish of a thief hanging from a cross (see Luke 23:42). Three men, each hanging from a cross, dying together—two were criminals; the other was Jesus. And the only thing more scandalous and outrageous than the thief's plea is Jesus' unwavering promise that he'd remember him.

The worth and splendor that Jesus sees in the life of a seemingly worthless and insignificant person is truly a divine mystery. The unrestricted love of God cannot be contained or comprehended.

God's love is immense and vast. So much so that it'd be easier to contain all of the world's oceans in a tiny cup than to comprehend the love in God's heart for each one. Truthfully, there is no more mind-boggling thing in the world than the scandalous reality of God's love. The simple fact that God loves me as much as he loves Jesus seems crazy to me.

At times the stories told by women and men whose hearts have been seized by the mighty power of God's scandalous affection have nearly taken my breath away. Years ago, "during what began as a long and lonely hour of prayer," writes Brennan Manning, "I heard in faith Jesus Christ say, 'For love of you I left My Father's side. I came to you who ran from Me, fled Me, who did not want to hear My name. For love of you I was covered with spit, punched, beaten, and affixed to the wood of the cross.'"

Can you fathom the impact of such an encounter on you? Manning continues, "These words are burned on my life. Whether I am in a state of grace or disgrace, elation or depression, that night of fire quietly burns on. I looked at the crucifix . . . figuratively saw the blood streaming . . . and heard the cry of His wounds: 'This isn't a joke. It is not a laughing matter to Me that I have loved you.' The longer I looked the more I realized that no man has ever loved me and no one could love me as He did."

Can you imagine the transformation that would occur as a result of such an encounter? "I learned that night," Manning said, "what a wise old man had told me years earlier: 'Only the one who has experienced it can know what the love of Jesus Christ is. Once you have experienced it, nothing else in the world will seem more beautiful or desirable.'"

Last summer I met a homeless gentleman while walking along a sidewalk in the city that's my home. Our conversation began with him asking a very simple and important question for any follower of Jesus. "Will you please help me?"

When I asked, "What kind of help do you need?" I was struck by the smallness of his request: "I've already got a cup, but could you pay someone to fill it?"

An hour later he was checked into a local motel, and just before leaving he asked me a question as bold and rich with meaning as his first had been. His question is one I'll carry with me and will never forget. How could I?

"Will you promise to always remember me?"

"I promise I will. Always." Every day I pray for grace to keep my promise.

PAUSE AND PONDER

- How's your memory? Are there memories that you cherish? Now's a good time to ponder what some of them are and why you cherish them.

- How's your memory? Are there memories that you run from and others you hide from? Now's a good time to ponder what some of them are and why you run or hide from them.

- Have you wondered whether you hide some memories that it'd be good for you to recover? Perhaps a conversation with God or a spiritual friend would be wise.

10 Throwing in the Towel on Religion

"I often wonder if religion is the enemy of God.
It's almost like religion is what happens when the
Spirit has left the building."

BONO

Throwing in the towel" is an expression commonly recognized as an acknowledgment of defeat. It comes from the boxing world, where a fighter indicates surrender by throwing a towel into the ring.

I don't typically think of myself as a "quitter." Ask anyone who knows me; I'm not one to *throw in the towel* quickly, eagerly or with ease. Some might say I'm stubborn, and I'd quickly add that's not all. I'm also arrogantly proud and foolishly determined to always look good. Nonetheless, when it comes to religion, my deepest regret is not throwing in the towel sooner.

Nothing I can think of has brought me more long-lasting relief, peace, gladness and deep inner healing than has throwing in the towel on *religion*. It's also renewed my hope for the future by liberating me from the burden of my failed past. In turn the Holy Spirit has occupied more space in my life, guiding me onto a path of greater freedom that enmeshment in religion would have never allowed. Yet most dramatic and effective: my union with God is becoming wildly intense in its intimacy, and my love for sacred Scripture, especially prayerfully savoring its living words and having the Spirit work them into my life, is dramatically transforming my life from the inside out. Therefore, I'm accepting myself as lovable more often because I know I am deeply, passionately and unconditionally loved by God.

Consequently, imagining me climbing into a boxing ring with a frightfully more formidable opponent and getting my brains scrambled is outrageously more appealing and less likely to destroy me than a return to religion. Religion is deceptively misleading; it appeals to our fallen nature and preys on our insatiable craving for control. It has an unsuccessful past and an insolvent future, and has been declared a loser. Anyone who reads the Bible without religious preconceptions can't help recognizing that religion wasn't needed in the Garden of Eden and there'll be no need for religion in heaven. Jesus died and was resurrected in order to convince the world that life in union with him is all he wants and all we need.

THE MOST DANGEROUS ENERGY SOURCE

I am utterly convinced that religion was invented in the devil's workshop. Worse still, the devil duped us into believing that we can't live without it. Demonstrating his skill at deception, the devil's sales pitch is enticing, appealing to our desire to be smart. Worst of all, the world cut a deal with the devil and took out the patent.

Now, thanks to Satan, everyone enters life with a proud, natural, uncontrollable urge. We all yearn to make our own life better. The theology of religion is simple and operates on a single tenet: *Exploit and marshal whatever power is obtainable to achieve whatever goal you believe is a smart endeavor.* Moral religion instructs that our quest can't interfere with others' interests. The general theme is to first make life better for yourself, and then others if you're able. That's religion in a nutshell. One of its essential features, making it rather enticing, is that it leaves narcissism, a fundamental commitment to our well-being above all other values, firmly in place.

Religion, "the self-absorbed search for a way to be in control of our own well-being," writes Larry Crabb, "is now the natural energy in every human soul." And what we've discovered (at least some have) is that rather than getting something we can't live without, religion got us. And now it's in charge. And it uses rules to force our steps, guilt to keep us in line and rituals to remind us of our failure to live up the rules. Meanwhile, guilt and shame compel us to strive endlessly to improve our performance or at least its appearance, while our hidden feelings of failure lead us into a private storm of weariness, hopelessness and despair. And because religion is the most deadly energy source known to humankind, it's killing us.

The tragedy of it lies in the fact that we were made for something far greater. We were designed for a lively *spiritual* journey with other pilgrims, while living in intimate union with God, the lover of our souls. Instead we're on an arduous *religious* journey, feeling isolated, lonely and afraid. Meanwhile it's robbing us of contentment and joy while promising an overflow. Even when it appears we're making progress, it's wearing us out or puffing us up.

What does Jesus see, what does Jesus think, how does Jesus feel when he gazes at you and me? Perhaps we'll gain a clue if we look at him. One day Jesus stood in front of a large crowd and saw people who were "harassed and helpless" (Matthew 9:36 NRSV). In all likelihood, they appeared to have their act together, yet Jesus saw an internal conflict between following religion and following God wreaking havoc in their souls. Jesus saw people striving to meet the religious requirements they'd been told were necessary for life to go well, and they were crumbling beneath the weight of

the impossible demands. Get with the program! Don't let up! Do
this! Do that! Don't stop! Here's the way to live, to make your marriage perfect, to make your kids behave, to make your depression
go away. Be kind to people, be nice and thoughtful. Hang in there.
Get busy! Try harder! Keep at it! You'll get it. If you just have faith
your life will work!

"Those were the lyrics" writes Larry Crabb, "to the music the
Pharisees played." And I know he's right because I've sung those
same songs and I've heard them sung in our families, in our busi-
nesses, in our schools and most tragically in our churches. We
have the right answers, quick and easy answers for everything.
Are your kids making you crazy or breaking your heart? The Bible
clearly holds the answer; do what it says. Is sex or money the problem in your marriage? Then adhere to these biblical principles.
Confused? Weary? Lonely? Depressed? Haunted by memories
from your past or fears about the future? Then let me tell you what
the problem is and how you can fix things. It's all religion and it's
all up to you.

Ever since the Garden of Eden, every living creature has been
the beneficiary of an inheritance. Tragically our bequest is a deadly
disease called religion. You and I experience its awful symptoms
daily. As Adam's child, we want control. Yet, as God's child, we
want God. What a devilish pickle we live in—natural desire com-
petes against supernatural desire. Religion and intimate union
with God are at war, and we're caught in the crossfire.

An Indelible Mark

Occasionally we encounter someone whose life leaves an indelible
mark on our life. We might sense the likelihood early on, or we
might remain unaware for quite some time. The contexts often
vary. The person may be family or a close friend, or our contact
with him or her may be less direct. The indelible mark may come

as we listen to the person's voice or see him or her on a stage or screen, or it might come while reading a book or magazine.

As I began reading *The End of Religion*, I recognized early on that author Bruxy Cavey's written words were going to leave some kind of mark on my life. The first clue appeared in the introduction, where he acknowledged that *Monty Python and the Holy Grail* was one of the funniest movies he'd seen.

I recall laughing out loud as he retold a favorite scene: King Arthur and company use the "Holy Hand Grenade" to blow up the nasty bunny with big teeth. From the moment he expressed his belief that the "Holy Hand Grenade" could apply to the Bible, which he portrayed as a document designed to "blow up religion from the inside out, with the teachings of Jesus functioning as the pin," his life had already begun marking mine. When he invited his readers to begin considering each time they picked up their Bible that they were holding an explosive device, I felt like I might explode. Brilliant!

My religious orientation left me feeling that the Bible was a dud, a religious textbook filled with boring, irrelevant history. When it was explosive, it was blowing up in my face, casting images of an angry, disgusted God. What I've since encountered is the Bible's radical message and its power to dismantle religion's grip on anyone who reads it without religious preconceptions. I've realized that the Bible is alive. It's a living collection of God-inspired writings pointing toward a surprisingly nonreligious intimacy with God that eventually culminates in the subversive message and mission of Jesus. Embraced by religious institutions, it nonetheless propagates an *irreligious* agenda, one designed for dismantling religion from the inside out. Reading the Bible now, with heightened interest in Jesus' agenda, I understand more clearly my former mindless addiction to religion.

Understanding religion's values and functions, it becomes appar-

ent that religious laws and rituals, systems and institutions are neither the Bible's starting nor ending point. The Bible begins with the
portrayal of a perfect world. Read without religious bias, it's easier
to recognize that it was a world *without* religion. In the Garden, God
and people are free to live in freedom, peace and intimacy.

Remembering God's original intent provides proper perspective. Reading the Bible without religious prejudice, we see that
religion's traditions and rituals, rules and routines were given after people turned from God's ideal. The stuff that religion gives us,
the rules and rituals, regulations and routines are like a map leading to a priceless treasure. Yet this distinction is essential: *they are
not the treasure.* This is the truth Jewish poet and philosopher
Abraham Joshua Heschel was making when he said, "Religion as
an institution, the Temple as an ultimate end, or, in other words,
religion for religion's sake, is idolatry." However, religion's emphasis on the rules and rituals and regulations and routines is so
enormous that its followers wind up confusing the treasure map
for the treasure. My darkest fear is that religious oppression has
broken the spirit of some treasure-seekers, leaving them incapable
of believing the treasure could be theirs.

The closing chapters of the Bible indicate that God is ultimately
leading the world back to the Garden, where religious rules, rituals, institutions and instruction are not needed. Following John's
sneak peek of heaven, he recorded his observations, and I can't
help wondering what the reaction of the listening crowd was as
John revealed his vision: "I saw no temple in the city." The temple
was the institution that connected people with God in first-
century Israel. It was the focal point of their faith. The temple
represented the presence of God. Is it possible that John failed to
notice that particularly significant portion of the celestial tour?

No, John didn't overlook seeing the temple, instead he explains
what not seeing a temple meant: "I saw no temple in the city, for

its temple is the Lord God the Almighty and the Lamb" (Revelation 21:22 NRSV). In this brave new world God himself will be our temple, our sacred space. No more rules, no more formulas, no more structures, no more rituals, no more treasure map to lead us to the treasure that is God.

THE STORY THE BIBLE TELLS

The story the Bible tells is about our legacy of endless mistakes. It includes details about detours, sidetracks, washed-out roads, crashes, losing the keys, conflicts with traveling companions, running out of gas and so on. Meanwhile, it's also a story about God's scandalous persistence, patience and kindness, fueled by limitless love helping us along the way. In the end it's the story of God not only revealing a solution but actually becoming the solution himself, not just standing in the roadway pointing the way but becoming the way. And God's destination is back to the Garden. This is the meaning and mission of Jesus.

Between the beginning and the end the Bible presents a subplot about our pathetic response to religion's rules and routines. Religion naturally fixates on the subplot because it's all about us. But God sees it in its proper light, and continually brings us back to the main plot of the Bible, which is the coming of Jesus, whose intentions are apparent. His plan is to put an end to religion and point the way back to an ideal home. This explains in a nutshell why I stand with others doggedly insisting that seeing the Bible as a "Holy Hand Grenade" is fitting since it invites us into a way of living that exposes religion's lethal powers and the ultimate truth that it's unnecessary.

Religion kept me from seeing Jesus as he truly is. However, since throwing in the towel I see him more clearly and understand more fully religion's reaction. Jesus is scandalously unruly and appears dangerously out of control. It's no wonder that religious forces would conspire to domesticate Jesus and herald him the founder and president of a global religion. But religion is wrong and foolish to use the devil's tricks, because all attempts fail. Jesus refuses to be boxed, caged, captivated, tamed or temple-broken. Jesus is the challenger and corrector of all religions. He's a subversive, anti-institutional revolutionary who exposes religion and its institutions as an even greater threat than the devil.

Yet saying Jesus is "anti-institutional" doesn't mean Jesus opposes all forms of organization. Jesus was present in the beginning when the Spirit hovered over the formless void and darkness, bringing order and beauty to the world. Nonetheless, Jesus opposes dependence on any organization for our connection with God. Thus "the primary mission of Jesus was to tear down religion as the foundation for people's connection with God and to replace it with Himself." When this part of his purpose grips us, the New Testament writings in particular are seen in a totally different light. His stories, the confrontations, even the healings are seen in an enlightened and illumined way.

I'd like to invite you to do something that will take only a few minutes. However, I feel confident it will be meaningful and perhaps an enlightening exercise. Take a piece of paper and spend three to five minutes writing down every word that comes to mind when you hear the name Jesus. Do it now.

Now reflect on each word. Be with the word and let it be with you. What do you see? What feelings rise to the surface? It wouldn't surprise me to hear you say you're surprised by a new insight or emotion. I'd expect you to experience a familiar emotion or to revisit a moment in your life that you associate with Jesus' name. I hope you realize how vital these thoughts and feelings are. Nothing possesses greater power to twist and deform or to straighten and reform our soul than our view of God. Meanwhile, I can't help imagining that the word *irreligious* didn't make it onto many lists.

There was certainly a time when it wouldn't have made mine. But those days are long gone.

A major influence when I decided to throw in the towel on religion was the realization that the Jesus portrayed in the Bible is far more appealing, dynamic and real than the meek, mild and domesticated Jesus my religion promoted. "The people who hanged Christ," writes Dorothy Sayers, "never, to do them justice, accused Him of being a bore; on the contrary, they thought Him too dynamic to be safe. It has been left for later generations to muffle up that shattering personality and surround Him with an atmosphere of tedium."

FROM HOLY WATER TO WEDDING WINE

One of my favorite miracle stories in the Bible is when Jesus attended a wedding and turned water into quality wine. Numerous things about the story stir my imagination and remind me of qualities in Jesus that I admire. A particular trait is how Jesus used his power not only to heal but also to celebrate life. I can't resist believing that Jesus was as playful as he was prayerful.

However, there is something in this story, a scandal, that I overlooked for a long time. But it's made up for lost time, holding me captive since I discovered it a while ago. I'd like you to look for it yourself. But first, I'll give you a hint: look beyond the wine. Here's another hint: Jesus often did things that won the admiration of common folks, while at the same time infuriating the religious elite. I believe it's a trait that Jesus values so much that he imparts it to his followers. Proof oozes during those moments when sinful, broken, hurting people are pleasantly surprised at how accepting followers of Jesus are. There's also proof of what's bad about religion, when religious people are furious at how accepting Jesus' followers are. I'm convinced that when those moments occur it's because we've begun to realize the difference between *agreement* and *acceptance*. Predictably it's a distinction that religious people find difficult to understand and Jesus views as being essential.

One more thing: please read the story slowly several times and relax. One of the significant changes that have occurred since I threw in the towel on religion is less stress. It's helped me realize that it never helps to be in a hurry or to be concerned with results when I read Scripture. That's God's responsibility. My part is to keep showing up and opening myself to God. I've begun to cherish the wisdom in this simple approach to reading the Bible: "If you read quickly, it will benefit you little. You will be like a bee that merely skims the surface of a flower. Instead, in this new way of reading with prayer, you must become as the bee who penetrates into the depths of the flower. You plunge deeply within to remove its deepest nectar." I'm also realizing that each word in the Bible possesses immense power and is filled with countless mysteries that only the Holy Spirit is familiar with and is able to impart. And it seems that when I'm peaceful and relaxed and trusting God to say whatever God pleases, more happens.

Three days later there was a wedding in the village of Cana in Galilee. Jesus' mother was there. Jesus and his disciples were guests also. When they started running low on wine at the wedding banquet, Jesus' mother told him, "They're just about out of wine."

Jesus said, "Is that any of our business, Mother—yours or mine? This isn't my time. Don't push me."

She went ahead anyway, telling the servants, "Whatever he tells you, do it."

Six stoneware water pots were there, used by the Jews for ritual washings. Each held twenty to thirty gallons. Jesus ordered the servants, "Fill the pots with water." And they filled them to the brim.

"Now fill your pitchers and take them to the host," Jesus said, and they did.

When the host tasted the water that had become wine (he didn't know what had just happened but the servants, of course, knew), he called out to the bridegroom, "Everybody I know begins with their finest wines and after the guests have had their fill brings in the cheap stuff. But you've saved the best till now!"

This act in Cana of Galilee was the first sign Jesus gave, the first glimpse of his glory. And his disciples believed in him. (John 2:1-11)

Two of our three children have gotten married in the past couple of years, so I've seen some remarkable wedding gifts. However, six huge jars filled with quality wine, especially when you're running out, is a gift that exceeds any I've seen. John too is impressed. I'd have to commend him for his attention to detail. (I suspect it might be a quality Jesus brought out in him.) John makes note of the fact that these stone water jars could each hold between twenty and thirty gallons. Now we're talking about a lot of wine, between 120 and 180 gallons. That's enough to fill over two thousand four-ounce glasses. Already Jesus seems to be making a subtle statement about generosity, abundance and providing enough for everyone. But remember, this is just the beginning.

Now let me call to your attention a word with special significance in the final verse. In most translations the word is *miracle*, yet in the version provided here the word is more accurately translated *sign*, which refers to something that points toward the true nature of Jesus' message and mission. This miracle or sign is not just about providing refreshment for thirsty guests and celebrating the bride and groom's marriage. There's much more going on.

Consider the dramatic symbolism involved in the wedding

event. The notion of miraculously turning water into a completely different liquid was familiar to the people at this celebration. As Jews, they were intimately acquainted with the story of Moses, who was given the power to turn water into blood (see Exodus 4:9), a symbol of God's judgment. Now Jesus comes possessing the power to turn water into wine, a symbol of God's blessing and joy (see Psalm 104:14-15). There's a subtle shift occurring with dramatic results. In the Hebrew Scriptures, which were written centuries before Jesus' arrival on earth, God had forecast that one day he would provide a prophet "like" Moses (Deuteronomy 18:18). Moses and Jesus both offered people freedom from whatever enslaved them, whether Egypt on the one hand or a deeper slavery than political oppression—slavery to our own sin and selfishness, and slavery to religion. Moses achieved freedom for God's people through manifestations of God's anger and judgment. Jesus offered it by demonstrating God's abundant grace and mercy. This doesn't mean that God as revealed by Moses and by Jesus is at odds or contradictory. Just as parenting styles change when children mature and circumstances change, God's response changes according to our development and contexts.

Certainly it isn't out of the ordinary to recognize that Jesus' message was dripping with blessing and joy. But through this "sign" Jesus wasn't *adding* to established religious tradition, he was subverting it. Did you recognize the scandal? It's okay if you missed it. I'm about to tell you anyway.

It's neatly hidden in verse 6. John is careful to note that Jesus didn't have the wine served out of normal wine jars. Instead he instructed the servants to use the sacred vessels reserved for a religious ritual. You see, one of the religious traditions of some groups, certainly including the Pharisees, was ritual hand-cleansing. (The Pharisees, you might recall, busted Jesus and his disciples for their failure to take seriously this ritual.) It consisted of a ceremonial dipping of their hands in sacred water as a way of symbolizing a desire to remain pure from the sin in the world (see Mark 7:1-4).

So the big question is, why would Jesus use these sacred stone vessels for serving the water-turned-to-wine? Obviously there were other containers available that could have been used. If they'd run out of wine, there would have been plenty of "empties," I'd think, to hold the wine. So why use the ceremonial vessels? Why use the vessels that were symbols of religious tradition? Why intentionally do something so likely offensive?

Others may differ, however I'm convinced that it was another crucial and illuminative sign. By means of Jesus' first miracle, he intentionally desecrates a highly valued religious symbol. He strategically and purposely chooses these sacred symbols to confront the religious system by converting them from symbols of personal purification into symbols of relational and gracious celebration. Jesus turns the tables and shifts the values from holy water to wedding wine. From legalism to living. From empty religion to deep and full relationship.

Jesus is giving a sign of things to come by saying that his gospel of radically accepting grace is too wonderful and different to be contained in and served from the old ways of religious form and tradition. The new wine that he's intending to serve calls for new containers (see Matthew 9:17).

When I began seriously considering throwing in the towel on religion, I knew it would necessitate letting go of and tearing myself away from religious assumptions and traditions in order to let Jesus be who the Bible says he is. I realized I could no longer allow two thousand years of church history and institutional prejudices and human agendas to tell me what he should be. Thus began my deliberate search for the authentic three-dimensional Jesus, beyond the modern-day symbols of the religion that bears his name.

The compelling desire that finally drove me to throw in the towel was my yearning to learn more about and from Jesus, who probably thinks our world needs more wine and less religion. What surprised me most have been the things I've had to unlearn. Now, a few years removed from this discovery and having experienced countless other things pertaining to Jesus' character, values and mission, I'm aware that I've only begun exploring the tip of the irreligious iceberg contained within the Bible. The writers of the four biblical books that record the earthly life of Jesus use a captivating Greek word to portray the effect that Jesus routinely had on his religious audiences. They describe Jesus as a *skandalon*, meaning a "stumbling rock," an offense, a scandal. My life offers proof that anyone who clings tightly to his or her religious presumptions will sooner or later become offended by Jesus. Unless, of course, they follow the example of countless people who are living in the illusion that they have domesticated the wild Jesus of the Bible and squeezed him into a tightly sealed box.

Thankfully, the biblical record is living and therefore won't allow Jesus' irreligious agenda to be so easily confined or dismissed. His subversive spirituality reflects a manner of living that he was willing to die to preserve. And through his death Jesus finally brought about the end of religion.

FAITHFULLY GOING TO CHURCH

Imagine someone faithfully going to church out of a sense of duty. As far back as they can remember, going to church is what they were supposed to do. Often they'd sit in church looking around wondering, *Is this really what God had in mind? Does this truly reflect what matters most to God? Is this what God really wants from me?*

Occasionally a Scripture lesson like this one would be read:

Then Jesus said to the crowds and to his disciples, "The

scribes and the Pharisees sit on Moses' seat; therefore, do whatever they teach you and follow it; but do not do as they do, for they do not practice what they teach. They tie up heavy burdens, hard to bear, and lay them on the shoulders of others; but they themselves are unwilling to lift a finger to move them. They do all their deeds to be seen by others; for they make their phylacteries broad [boxes containing scriptural passages worn on the head and arm]. . . . They love to have the place of honor at banquets and the best seats in the synagogues, and to be greeted with respect in the marketplaces, and to have people call them rabbi." (Matthew 23:1-7 NRSV)

While listening, they'd ponder Jesus' words, thinking, *Isn't the meaning clear? Wasn't Jesus saying, "When being religious becomes more important to you than me, then everything will begin to revolve around your appearance and reputation. You love to be regarded highly. You crave respect. You love the best seat in the house where everyone can see you. It's all about image. How things look to other people."* Yet the worship service would end without resolving the inner turmoil. They'd leave not knowing what to do or how to feel about their relationship with God. They'd wonder whether they were as religious as they should be.

On rare occasions a harsher passage of Scripture would be read, and they'd feel even more deeply troubled.

I've had it with you! You're hopeless, you religion scholars, you Pharisees! Frauds! Your lives are roadblocks to God's kingdom. You refuse to enter, and won't let anyone else in either. (Matthew 23:13)

Then they'd think about modern-day illustrations of the same thing Jesus described: religious people abusing their positions of authority and actually getting in the way of other people who are sincerely searching for God. Sometimes they'd wander into a question like whether it's possible to be interested in a friendship with Jesus but at the same time be turned off by religion.

Once in a while they'd notice something in the news about the drastic increase in the number of Americans who don't go to church. And instead of being startled by the news or critical of the people who'd stopped going to church, they'd feel that somehow they understood why. Although they were aware of their resistance to their sometimes more intimate and real and reflective questions, they'd still stop and ask, *Why do I do what I do? Is it to keep the peace? Is it to keep from making waves, disappointing others or possibly causing people to think less of me? Is it so that I don't feel guilty?*

Can you relate to any of those thoughts or feelings? Could this person I'm describing be you? Are you, like me, sometimes troubled when Jesus states in certain terms that God doesn't want or even give a flip about meaningless religious rituals? Does focusing on what matters most to God alarm you even more? What about the fact that God wants your heart? Does it frighten you knowing that giving God your heart completely will completely change your heart? What do you feel when you imagine yourself caring about the things God cares most about?

One of the clearest things to me about God is how much he hates it when I put on a religious show and then turn around and ignore the things that matter most to him. Most especially, he can't stand it when I ignore the poor, the broken, the marginalized and the oppressed.

GOD'S RELENTLESS AFFECTION
Organic awareness of God's relentless affection, with its remarkable power to change our life, always requires surrender on a scale that appears to some like an enormous waste. For this reason, Thomas Merton wrote that "we must know the truth, we must

love the truth we know, and we must act according to the measure of our love. Truth is God himself who cannot be loved apart from surrender to his will." This kind of knowing insists on a response that results in our willingness to be touched by God's distinctive love. There is no touch in the world with greater power to change our life than God's touch. Abandonment to God's love is the way we find the home for which our souls most deeply yearn and the power to touch the lives of others in a healing way.

Nothing is more remarkable to see in the entire world than the transformation that occurs when divine love touches a willing heart. Thus it follows that for me there is certainly nothing more humbling than having the privilege of observing it in each of our three children. For instance, when our younger son was thirteen, he and my wife traveled with me to a youth workers' convention, where I was on the program. During one of the plenary sessions, a video portrayed the most profound "out of sight, out of mind" atrocity ever known to humankind. The trials and suffering of those living in HIV-stricken Africa had then become the greatest humanitarian disaster of our time.

More than fourteen million children had then lost one or both parents to the AIDS pandemic. Many more were left vulnerable as family resources were stretched thin to care for these orphans. Then it was estimated that by 2010 the number of orphans would more than double to twenty-five million. The video posed the simple question: "Who is caring for these orphans?" The answer was quite disturbing. Extended family members, often aging grandparents, were the only ones left to care for them. This overwhelming financial burden made the task of caring for and educating the orphans almost impossible.

Entire families of children were trying to make it all alone. They struggled to grow their own food, and often, instead of going to school, they worked long hours at backbreaking jobs for pennies. Precious lives hung in the balance.

Most of these children were not infected with HIV/AIDS. However, they were malnourished or sick and vulnerable to exploitation. Every day was a struggle for survival. Older siblings were forced to drop out of school in order to take care of younger siblings. These innocent children, still grieving over the loss of their parents, were forced to function as adults.

After the video ended, a practical, tangible way to get involved and take a stand against the AIDS pandemic was introduced. By joining the "One Life Revolution," we could participate in a fight that could quite literally save an entire generation from the horrific effects of HIV/AIDS—and change the course of history.

The rally cry was simple: "You have one life—Do something!"

Lee, sitting next to his mom, looked up into her eyes and declared, "I've got to do something!" The next thing she knew, he was standing in a long line with hundreds of youth workers waiting to receive his "kit" of information. Ever since, Lee's been actively taking a stand. It's abundantly clear that he, like many other young followers of Jesus, is tired of people retreating from the things that matter most to God. They're tired of being told they can't do enough to solve the problem, therefore they need to be cautious, avoid risks and wait patiently. Lee told me his interpretation of what he most sees in the church is, "Don't waste your time, efforts or money on hopeless causes."

Thank God, his generation is sick and tired of waiting and worrying about whether their efforts to assist others are a waste or a beautiful thing. They want to do something. Now. They want to get their hands dirty, empty their pockets, and sacrifice their time and energy to touch innocent victims—vulnerable children and widows—with help and hope.

The particular thing I've grown to admire most about Lee's faith, and those who are like him, is that it's much more narrowly focused on relationships than doctrine. He seems to understand that God is more intimately experienced in right relationships than in right beliefs. If you think about it, the concept is rather simple. After all, would you rather know things about your greatest hero or spend an evening together?

VITAL DISTINCTIONS

Living in intimate union with God is the fruit of vital distinctions. For example, a lot of people confuse religion with God and walk away from them both, which saddens God's heart. The point is neither religion nor Christianity. The point is being in intimate union with God. It means being a follower of Jesus. It's being connected with everything that matters to him, and those things are true and right and good.

There's an ancient story about a person whose deepest longing was to live in intimate union with God, and thus he wished to know what habits of the heart and mind were essential. One day he approached a wise and holy hermit and posed the question to him.

Without hesitation the hermit replied, "If you wish to live in intimate union with God, there are two things you must know: The first is that all of your efforts are of no avail."

"And the second," the disciple insisted.

"The second is that you must live as if you did not know the first."

Clearly, great pursuers of the spiritual life understand that the secret of the spiritual life is to live it until it becomes real. Yet one of the mysteries of the spiritual life is that it is not something that is gotten by merely wishing or hoping or striving or assuming. The spiritual life requires serious and sincere discipline. It is to be learned. It must be internalized. That is not to say that there's a formulaic set of steps or neatly arranged and numbered exercises to follow. It's a way of living, an attitude our mind adopts and an orientation our soul adapts itself to. And it's especially important to understand that this life is obtained by walking with Jesus and observing how he does it until no rules remain necessary. That's right, until there is no need for any rules.

A few summers ago my wife and I were vacationing on the North Carolina coast. We had eaten lunch when Lucie announced her plans to take an afternoon nap. Meanwhile, I headed for the door saying, "I'm going to work on my tan." Immediately I heard her snicker, so, spinning around quickly, I asked her, "Why did you snicker?"

"Oh, I didn't snicker," she responded innocently.

"Yes you did. I heard you. What did I say that was so funny?"

"Well, if you insist. When you said that you were 'going to *work* on your tan' I couldn't help wondering, *Where does the 'work' come in?*"

Capable of being defensive on the best of days, I began my argument: "Well for starters, I have at least two hundred yards to walk, and it's terribly hot. I have to carry a chair, and you don't just plop down anywhere. You have to pay attention to the angle of the sun. Then there's getting undressed and applying the lotion." To be truthful, I impressed myself with my well-reasoned rebuttal, that is, until she turned again and began heading for the bedroom, saying through her laughter as she walked, "You head on back to work then. But don't get too tired! What you're going to do certainly sounds like difficult work."

If I had to declare a winner, I'd say it was a tie. We were both correct. She was correct in implying that there was not much work involved. I was correct when I insisted that there was work involved. And so it is in the spiritual realm. We must learn to do those things that we've been given to do until we do them quite naturally.

As silly as it may sound, I'm suggesting that we must do those things that deepen and sustain our intimacy of relationship with

God until they become second nature. Just as there are essential things that must be done for our physical life to be sustained, things we don't rely on rules to accomplish (such as eating, sleeping and breathing), there are also things that must be done for our spiritual life to be sustained: we pray, we worship, we ponder Scripture, and we offer service to others. And we must do them until they become so natural to us that we no longer need rules.

WITH, IN AND FOR

The life God uniquely designed for us to live and for which our hearts naturally yearn cannot be achieved by means of our own effort, no matter how disciplined we may be. Instead it comes only by way of a few prepositions, *with, in* and *for*, what Eugene Peterson calls "prepositional participation." These prepositions join us to God and God's action. They are essentially the ways and means of being in on and participating in what God is doing.

It's essential for our experience and central to our understanding that we trust God and remain assured that we are neither now nor ever alone; we can trust that God is *with* us always: "'Look, the virgin shall conceive and bear a son, and they shall name him Emmanuel,' which means, 'God is with us'" (Matthew 1:23 NRSV). Furthermore, Jesus is *in* us: "I have been crucified with Christ; and it is no longer I who live, but it is Christ who lives in me. And the life I now live in the flesh I live by faith in the Son of God, who loved me and gave himself for me" (Galatians 2:19-20 NRSV). Finally, we can trust that God is *for* us: "What then are we to say about these things? If God is for us, who is against us?" (Romans 8:31 NRSV). *With, in* and *for*. These are the authoritative connecting, enabling, relationship-forging words that set us on the course God designed us to follow.

Thus, as I live these days in relationship with Jesus, no longer looking to religion for anything, I'm naturally given things to be-

lieve and do, but in that doing, it's never intended for me to become the subject, nor am I to perform in order to live in intimate
union with God. Instead I'm set free from that life-crushing burden that I was never supposed to carry. It belongs to God, just as I
do and just as we all do. Thanks be to God. Amen.

Notes

Special Note

I have benefited from numerous readings and conversations with individuals regarding why I use the masculine pronoun when writing and speaking of God. I made this decision with conviction and regret combined. The dilemma is due to the lack of a gender-neutral third-person pronoun in the English language. English simply lacks a singular personal pronoun that transcends our categories of gender. When referring to God it is not an option to use plural pronouns, as we can when speaking of human beings. Biblical revelation makes clear that God is one. The impersonal pronoun "it" is not a reasonable option given the personal nature of God. Repeating the noun "God" when the sentence structure calls for a pronoun is also unacceptable. Thus I have discerned that there is no other acceptable choice than to use the pattern set by reliable biblical scholars. In so doing, I feel I'm being faithful in my confession of God's personhood. Meanwhile, God, who is wholly other than us, transcends the distinctions of our human sexuality.

Chapter 1: Is Your Faith in God or Religion?

page 30   "The Messiah is the one": Barbara Brown Taylor, "Jesus Talks (Exodus 17:1-7; Romans 5:1-11; John 4:5-42)," *The Christian Century*, February 12, 2008, p. 19.

page 31   *prodigal* doesn't mean "wayward": *Merriam-Webster's Collegiate Dictionary*, s.v. "prodigal."

page 35   "Greyhound Bitterly Disappointed After Finally Catching Mechanical Rabbit," *TheBrushback.com*, June 22, 2003 <www.thebrushback.com/Archives/Archives/greyhound_full.htm>.

Chapter 2: The Myth That Jesus Thinks Like Us

pages 39-40 "Christianity has become bloated": David Kinnaman, *unChristian: What a New Generation Really Thinks About Christianity*

. . . *and Why It Matters* (Grand Rapids: Baker, 2007), p. 15. In my opinion, this is an eye-opening book that brilliantly unpacks the major criticisms of "outsiders" leveled against Christians. It offers insight into why those negative images exist and how we can more effectively represent Jesus to the outsiders' world.

page 42   "I prefer to be true to myself": Frederick Douglass, *Narratives of the Life of Frederick Douglass, An American Slave* (1845; reprint, New York: Barnes & Noble Classics, 2003).

page 47   "this is not a man you want teaching": Barbara Brown Taylor, "Something About Jesus," *The Christian Century*, April 3, 2007, p. 43.

page 50   "the Maker of all things shrank down": Philip Yancey, *The Jesus I Never Knew* (Grand Rapids: Zondervan, 1995), p. 36.

page 57   "A great man knows he is not God": G. K. Chesterton, *The Everlasting Man* (New York: Dodd, Mead, 1925), p. 204.

Chapter 3: Beauty in Brokenness

page 69   God and the Indian earthquake: Leonard Pitts, "God Knows, Suffering Is Part of Game," *Miami Herald*, February 3, 2001.

page 73   "Their hearts are already broken": Barbara Brown Taylor, *Context: Martin E. Marty on Religion and Culture*, January 2006, Part B, p. 4. Reprinted from an article that appeared first in *The Living Pulpit*, "The Evils of Pride and Self-Righteousness," October-December 2005, p.5.

page 75   "Forget your perfect offering": Leonard Cohen, quoted in Anne Lamott, *Traveling Mercies* (New York: Anchor, 2000), p. 40.

page 80   The notion of "*Reader's Digest* selves" originates with Mike Yaconelli.

Chapter 4: What's a Picture Worth?

page 93   the naive plumber and Niagara Falls: Anthony De Mello, *Taking Flight: A Book of Story Meditations* (New York: Doubleday, 1988), p. 105.

page 99   not "the believing parts but the beholding parts": Barbara Brown Taylor, *Leaving Church: A Memoir of Faith* (San Francisco: HarperSanFrancisco, 2006), pp. 109-10.

page 100   "We tend to live as though our lives would go on forever": Frederick Buechner, *The Hungering Dark* (New York: HarperCollins, 1969), pp. 72-73.

Chapter 5: Right Rules or Right Relationship?

page 112   "bedraggled, beat-up, burnt-out": Brennan Manning, *The Rag-amuffin Gospel: Good News for the Bedraggled, Beat-up, and Burnt Out* (Portland, Ore.: Multnomah, 1990), p. 12.

page 112   Some may read this section and think that I came down too hard on the Pharisees, or came down on them for the wrong reasons. On the other hand, some may conclude that I hit the nail on the head. Regardless, I have thoughtfully and prayer-fully considered the perspective of numerous scholars regarding the religion of the Pharisees. At the same time, and without apology, the basis for my opinion is rooted primarily in my own reading and understanding of Scripture, not least the sayings of Jesus.

I've given particular attention (and, I pray, with genuine openness) to the claims of "new perspective" theologians who believe that many chief concerns of the Protestant Reformation were either incorrect or ill-directed. In a nutshell, its advocates maintain that first-century Judaism has been misunderstood and therefore the apostle Paul's writings have been seriously misinterpreted. Specifically, they insist that Judaism in Paul's day (obviously meaning Jesus' day too) was not a works-based religion. Instead they maintain that it was a covenant-based religion in which works played a prominent role. While some critics of the "new perspective" acknowledge that their portrayal of Judaism may be exaggerated, they remain convinced that Judaism was a religion of works.

Meanwhile I'm arriving at a few beliefs of my own. First, while the advocates and critics of the "new perspective" remain determined to prove their correctness, both sides appear reactionary and thus one-sided in their argument, prone to exaggerate and unwilling to listen. In my experience that's always been a byproduct of religion. (While I find nothing offensive about the focus of the debate, its manner and style is so. It belongs, in my opinion, to the kinds of religion Jesus opposed.) Garry Wills concludes his portrayal of those kinds of religion with this observation: "If that sounds like just about every form of religion we know, then we can see how far from religion Jesus stood" (Garry Wills, *What Jesus Meant* [New York: Penguin, 2006], p. 7).

Second, as this book asserts, I believe that all religion bears the same fatal flaw. All religion is based on something we must do. Jesus' death and resurrection and the Holy Spirit's subsequent arrival are signs that God is not in the business of religion. Therefore I stand in solidarity with John Stott who writes: "There is nothing meritorious about faith. . . . Nor is salvation a sort of cooperative enterprise between God and us. . . . No, grace is non-contributory, and faith is the opposite of self-regarding. The value of faith is not to be found in itself, but entirely and exclusively in its object, namely Jesus Christ and him crucified. To say 'justification by faith alone' is another way of saying 'justification by Christ alone.' Faith is the eye that looks to him, the hand that receives his free gift, the mouth that drinks the living water. As Richard Hooker, the late sixteenth-century Anglican divine, wrote: 'God justifies the believer—not because of the worthiness of his belief, but because of his worthiness who is believed" (John Stott, *The Message of Romans* [Downers Grove, Ill.: InterVarsity Press, 1994], pp. 117-18).

pages 115-16   "We think salvation belongs to the proper and pious": Brennan Manning, *The Ragamuffin Gospel*, pp. 23-24.

pages 117-18   "Grace is outrageously unfair": Michael Yaconelli, "Statement of Belief: Important Stuff Youth Specialties Believes," in *Michael Yaconelli: Selected Writings* (El Cajon, Calif.: Youth Specialties, 2003), p. 32.

pages 122-23   "We did not search you out": Vincent Donovan, *Christianity Rediscovered* (Maryknoll, N.Y.: Orbis, 2003), p. 48.

Chapter 7: Why This Waste?

page 148   "He really could've been a star": Chris Willman, quoted in Sarah Pulliam, "Larry Norman, 'Father of Christian Rock,' Dies at 60," *ChristianityToday.com*, February 26, 2008 <www.larrynorman.com/pdfs/Christianity_Today2.pdf>.

page 148   "I feel like a prize in a box of Cracker Jacks": Larry Norman, quoted in ibid.

page 151   "Houston, we have a problem": Wikipedia reports that though Lovell actually said, "Houston, we've had a problem," it has become widely misquoted in popular culture as "Houston, we have a problem." See <http://en.wikipedia.org/wiki/Apollo_13>.

pages 156-57   "Originally, I believed the acceptance of a loving God": Antony Campbell, *God First Loved Us* (Mahwah, N.J.: Paulist, 2001), p. 26.

pages 163-64 Philip Yancey wrote: Philip Yancey, "The Holy Inefficiency of Henri Nouwen," *Christianity Today*, December 9, 1996, p. 80.

Chapter 8: Doing What We Can

page 171 "starved for a good word": Garrison Keillor, *Lake Wobegon Days* (New York: Penguin, 1985), p. 323.

page 174 "Imagine, if you will": John de Graaf, David Wann and Thomas H. Naylor, *Affluenza: The All-Consuming Epidemic* (San Francisco: Berrett-Koehler, 2005), p. 1.

page 178 "Be who you is, 'cause if you ain't": Forrest Gump in the film *Forrest Gump*, dir. Robert Zemeckis, 142 min., Paramount Picures, 1994.

pages 178-79 One night an angel appeared: Brennan Manning, *Ruthless Trust: The Ragamuffin's Path to God* (San Francisco: HarperSanFrancisco, 2000), pp. 141-42.

page 180 "I never look at the masses as my responsibility": Mother Teresa, quoted in Michael Collopy, *Works of Love Are Works of Peace: Mother Teresa of Calcutta and the Missionaries of Charity* (San Francisco: Ignatius, 1996), p. 35.

page 181 "I am nothing. He is all": Mother Teresa, *My Life for the Poor*, ed. Jose Luis Gonzalez-Balado and Janet N. Playfoot (San Francisco: Harper & Row, 1985), p. 95.

page 182 In 1992 Dr. Graham was interviewed: Diane Sawyer interview with Billy Graham, "The Lion in Winter," viewed on WXII (Winston-Salem) on May 31, 2007.

Chapter 9: The Gift of Memory

page 189 "Memory believes before": William Faulkner, *Light in August*, (New York: Vintage, 1990), p. 119.

page 194 "It is not reserved for those who are well-known mystics": Jean Vanier, *Drawn into the Mystery of God Through the Gospel of John* (Mahwah, N.J.: Paulist, 2004), p. 296.

page 201 "all men are liars": Albert Bigelow Paine, *Mark Twain's Notebook* (New York: Harper & Brothers, 1935), p. 181.

page 207 conversation between Charles Ashworth and Father Darrow: Susan Howatch, *Glittering Images* (New York: Knopf, 1987). The dialogue is excerpted and adapted from pages 232-35.

page 208 according to psychologist and writer: Dan Allender, *The Wounded Heart* (Colorado Springs: NavPress, 1990), p. 15.

pages 208-9 "I was not angry with the people of Sighet": Elie Wiesel, *Leg-*

ends of Our Time (New York: Holt, Rinehart & Winston, 1968), pp. 123, 128.

page 210   "During what began": Brennan Manning, *The Signature of Jesus* (Old Tappan, N.J.: Chosen Books, 1988), p. 42.

Chapter 10: Throwing in the Towel on Religion

page 215   "the self-absorbed search for a way to be in control": Larry Crabb, *Soul Talk* (Brentwood, Tenn.: Integrity, 2003), p. 76.

page 216   "those were the lyrics": Ibid., p. 77.

page 218   "Religion as an institution": Abraham Joshua Heschel, *I Asked for Wonder* (New York: Crossroads, 1983), p. 40.

page 220   "the primary mission of Jesus was to tear down religion": Bruxy Cavey, *The End of Religion* (Colorado Springs: NavPress, 2007), p. 23.

page 221   "The people who hanged Christ": Dorothy L. Sayers, *Creed or Chaos? Why Christians Must Choose Either Dogma or Disaster* (Manchester, N.H.: Sophia Institute, 1974), pp. 6-7.

page 222   "If you read quickly": Madame Guyon, *Madame Guyon: Experiencing the Depths of Jesus Christ* (Goleta, Calif.: Christian Books, 1975), p. 16.

page 229   "we must know the truth": Thomas Merton, *The Ascent to Truth* (New York: Harcourt Brace, 1981), p. 8.